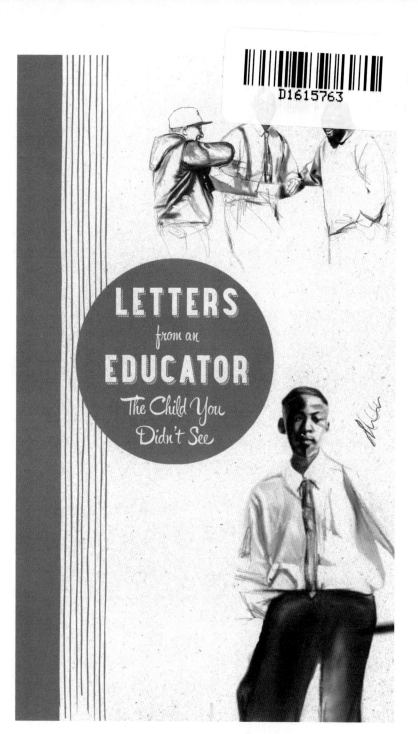

LETTERS
from an
EDUCATOR
The Child You Didn't See

John Broussard

If we have learned anything from Mandela and Martin,
it is that words are wings to the broken spirit. Thus, it becomes our
duty to lend ours to ensure everyone has the space needed to fly.

I'd like to dedicate this book to my family and all the amazing
friends, coaches, and mentors who have spoken light into my life.
In addition, I'd like to dedicate this book to all those who find
themselves constrained and conflicted by life's battles.
My wings I offer you. Let's fly together.

Contents

WHO DO YOU THINK YOU ARE?

*There comes a time when one must take a position that
is neither safe, nor politic, nor popular, but he must
take it because conscience tells him it is right.*

MARTIN LUTHER KING, JR.

I'm not sure there's a more intimidating room than one full
of coaches. The coaching profession overflows with ego and
moxie. It's a profession of uber-confident men and women who make
decisions for a living–not just decisions, but the *right* decisions, at
least in their own eyes.

And yet there I stood, a thirty-five-year-old African American
male in the middle of my second year as Athletic Director at Murrieta
Mesa High School. Staring back at me was something of a reflection
of our society, our country. I saw members of nationalities that did
not match my own, individuals of various ages and experience,
some of whom seemed to exude energies of "I have done this longer
than you—so just who do you think you are? The utter audacity!"

I had determined on this night to ignore the cutting eyes intent
on piercing my armor. I had a crucial message to deliver, and would
by any means necessary make my voice heard. I'd crafted it to be
intentionally raw, intentionally offensive, to those who represented
opposing, misguided principles.

Suppressing the tears in my eyes and lifting my heavy heart, I traded my sadness for the intense tone appropriate for my urgent plea. I glanced across the cold room on a dark, soundless night—disturbingly quiet, so silent that you could hear a feather drop. The muted room contrasted sharply with the negative thoughts that seemed to scream back at me from antagonistic faces around it.

But I would not back down. I'd seen enough. I'd heard enough. Like a boxer standing across the ring, I stared down my opponent. I wore a steely expression born of empathy: No flinch, no fear, zero hesitancy. I had arrived at this ring on this night ready to fight. Channeling every emotion, every experience, all the pain, neglect, and abuse I had ever known, I gathered my strength. My opponent had no chance. I was born for this.

My purpose is here, I thought. *My purpose is now.* From the depths of my soul, I bellowed out a monologue as if I were Dr. Martin Luther King, staring down the eyes of our nation's oppressors.

"I want you to understand something," I began. "I DO NOT SUPPORT COACHES. I support kids. If you support kids, then we are on the same team. But please understand me, I do not support coaches! I do not support your title; I support what your title represents. These walls, these buildings, me, none of this is here for our benefit. It's not about us. It's about kids. So, if you feel the need to curse at kids and disrespect kids, I don't support you.

"Athletics is an extension of the classroom. It's an educational environment. Imagine if I am in a classroom and a student answers a question incorrectly. If I were to respond by yelling, 'What the FUCK are you doing?!' I would look crazy as a teacher. It's not OK. That is not classroom management—so why is it OK on the court? On the field? It's not. Both are educational settings. So, if you feel it's OK to yell, 'What the *fuck* are you doing, we just got our ASS kicked,' as one of our athletes hugs an opposing player, a friend, at the conclusion of a game–then please, hear me clearly: I don't support you. We are not on the same team. You do not belong here. It's not the title I support, but the person holding the title."

I paused, regathered my strength, and continued. "What do you stand for? What character do you have? What . . . ." and on I went.

As you might imagine, it was a stirring scene—jarring and unsettling for some, spot-on and right on time for others. The truth is, Mesa is no different than your campus. It has amazing educators and coaches, but just like any campus, unhealthy habits sometimes reveal themselves. The dilemma reminds me of a Dr. King quote: "In the end, we will remember not the words of our enemies, but the silence of our friends." For me, the quiet boy who still keeps space inside me decided to contend out loud that day—*really* loud.

I will never forget that moment. But while I had planned to give that exact message in the explicit tone I gave it, I did not plan on the raw emotion that it brought out of me.

FLASHBACKS OF EMOTION

In the middle of my speech, the more I empathized with our students, I grew angrier, as if I were screaming out to the room, "These are *kids* we are talking about! Why are you hurting them?" As I spoke, I fought back the warm liquid welling up in the corners of my eyes while I thought about all the pain I had experienced as a child. I spoke with boldness and with a redemptive, advocating spirit, as if I were searching for the man who was supposed to protect the boy who still lives inside of me, the voiceless adolescent who experienced frightful levels of physical abuse, neglect, severe hunger, and a devastating lack of affection.

I wear these scars as I recommend that you wear yours: like a purple heart. In the military, soldiers recognized for outstanding courage in battle are awarded various medals. The purple heart is given to someone who has been injured in a fight or who has died.

My purple heart did not come from the military, because I found myself in a war for which I never enlisted. Who would ever willingly sign up for an embattled childhood? Nevertheless, I wear my purple heart with great honor, knowing that I have been wounded in battle, but recognizing that the weapons meant for my harm did not destroy me. In fact, the opposite has occurred. My painful journey has made me incredibly strong. It has given me life, and through that life, I am committed to helping save the lives of others.

It hasn't always been this way, of course. This has been a long, slow journey. The evolution of my spirit, from cowering to conquering, has been an internal pilgrimage where every bend of the road has proven to be a discovery filled with complexities. Even now, as I continue my career in child advocacy, hidden chapters and long-forgotten layers in my soul continually unspool.

I have written this book, not as an autobiography or personal history, but as a sign of hope. I have zero interest in writing a mere interest piece. For various reasons, I've hidden my story for many years. I've had to confront my past while trying to carve out the emotional space needed to see the battles within the young people I serve. Every day I confront the fierce opposition that our youth face, and together we fight against whatever energy opposes their brilliant selves.

This book is a vital voice for the unseen child who walks your campus daily, for the athlete who physically joins the huddle but emotionally runs routes alone. This is their playbook for you, offering a final shot at scholastic excellence for them. I write as both the trauma-inflicted student, as well as for you, the educator commissioned to leave no child behind.

I am learning that I cannot do this fully without entirely exposing my own pain, and that's what brings me back to my childhood. In the daily battles I face, I routinely channel difficult moments from my past. As I empathize with the painful emotions my students face, the same kind of emotions that confronted me many years ago as a child come rushing back.

Of course, this journey of mine is not unique to me. In fact, you and I are the same. I've never met anyone who hasn't experienced a certain level of agony or trauma. I think what separates individuals who live their life with laser-focused purpose, and those who wander aimlessly, is a matter of perspective.

WHAT DO YOU SEE?

I know that human experiences are and should be diverse. I have played basketball since fifth grade, for example, and on each of my teams I had a different role. The experiences and stories I tell about those days both echo and differ from those of my teammates and opponents, and that's OK. As a starter on some teams, my views likely vary from those of our twelfth man. As a wing player, my perspective on the team's offense surely produced different emotions than those of our center or point guard.

To change the image, imagine that you and I go on a bus tour together. As the tour guide, you take your spot at the front of the bus, to the right of the driver. No one sits in front of you; it's just you and the big front window displaying the wonders of the tour. I sit at the back of the bus, and in front of me sit fifty-four other passengers, which leaves me dealing with the noise and raucous behavior characteristic of such an environment. While all of us would probably agree that we experience the same tour, more than likely we will have contrasting experiences. My Yelp review will differ from your Yelp review. Visually, emotionally, even physically, we will describe the same ride in very different terms, mostly because we experience the tour from different seats. That's the beauty and uniqueness of life: we can walk together and alone at the same time, formulating what the universe means to us from our own, unique, singular perspectives.

So then, what hinders our acceptance of someone else's journey? I don't think it's necessarily that we judge their feelings as wrong, but rather that their experience may seem contrary to our own emotions or interpretations. We fail to realize that their views have been composed from their seat, not from ours. I've found it freeing and unifying to grow in accepting others' perspectives.

What our students face as their truth echoes the truths I have penned in this book. It's simply a journey or tour of life from my seat. The perspectives I expressed on certain issues "back then" reflected how I felt at that point in my life. I try hard to be self-aware enough to understand that my views of past experiences can evolve as I grow older and wiser, like my ever-changing clothing trends. My perspective on pain certainly has changed.

> *The deepest wounds*
> *Birth the deepest passions*
> *No remorse from darkness*
> *Without it*
> *This light inside of me never happens*
> Excerpt from *Diary of a Poet,* "Boys Weekend"

What we lack, most of the time, is empathy. We fail to understand or appreciate the world from another's very different viewpoint. Others see from *their* seat and understand through their tour of life.

Allow what you discover in the following chapters not to challenge your seat, but rather to expand your perspective. Let it grow just enough to help you see the children you serve through a sharper, clearer lens than ever before.

FROM EMPATHY TO HOPE

I have written this book from my own unique perspective, based on my vocation, my vehicle, and my lane. My vocation is child humanitarianism. My vehicle is education. And my lane for transformation is always the same: empathy.

In my experience, empathy is greater than, or at least equal to, equity. Empathy is the prequel that allows equity to exist. Empathy is the currency, while equity is the product. Without empathy, the attempt to create authentic equity will always be returned as "insufficient funds." The audience to whom you're trying to sell equity will see it as fraud, every single time.

This book is largely a lesson on empathy—why it's needed, where to find it, and how to win the whole child by keeping empathy activated inside *you*.

Empathy by itself, though, is never enough. It must lead somewhere, and the most important "somewhere" is hope. Hope is the one constant all of us need, regardless of our stage of life or personality. When we lose hope, we lose purpose, along with the vision to continue the journey. Hope, empowered by empathy, heals the brokenhearted. Acknowledging loss and finding words to soothe will always point to the core idea that progression is still possible. In fact, progression is still assured.

Empathy, working with hope, leads to resilience and the conviction that our darkest of nights will always be the prequel to the most amazing film script ever written. If you can embody that spirit in the middle of sharing a student's pain, then you will make things OK for the grievers, because they know the wave of emotion they feel now will always be followed by a calmer, warmer current.

Have you ever heard the Sam Cooke ballad, "A Change Is Gonna Come"? In many ways, it serves as the album cover for the American civil rights movement. The song has been preserved in the Library of Congress, with the National Recording Registry calling it "culturally and historically" important to our country. Written in 1964, it gives no definitive answers or solutions to the issues of equal rights, yet it stirred an entire nation. It provided hope in the face of extreme despair. It gave a strong voice to people otherwise ignored and embattled. It proved the power of words. The conviction of a few words, bellowed out through a microphone, both soothed and fueled our country during a time when visible hope was hard to come by.

If you are an educator, then you are the Sam Cooke of your classroom. You are the Dr. King of your locker room. It's your job to recognize the adversity of the moment and instill hope in young people in a way that screams, "A change is gonna come."

LET'S GO!

Now I'm ready to welcome you to *Letters from an Educator.* I frankly wish it becomes a flagship for child advocacy. I also hope that you view my experiences, not as a competing force to the idealism of any of my brethren, but rather as a view of life shaped through the eyes of a child who has seen hurt, felt loss, and found beauty. That same child, now an adult, continues to fight to discover and release purpose in all children, as well as in the adults who serve them.

I invite you on this journey for one reason. As I describe the burning passion I have for my calling in life—to help young people—my desire is that I can ignite in you a similar combustion of energy. As I search my soul, I anticipate that it will stir you to search yours, as well. And I hope that we both ask the universal question: *Why am I doing this?* I hope that by reading this book, you will rediscover and see the real WHY behind your career—and that by the time you finish, you will never unsee it again.

I expect our time together will feel emotional, heartbreaking, healing, and transformational. This literary journey with me may also serve as a journey within yourself. I promise you this: Purpose and passion await you, if you are willing to dig. If you are willing to do the work.

Let's go.

A CALL TO SERVE
OR A CALL TO INFLUENCE?

The two most important days of your life are the day
you were born and the day you find out why.

MARK TWAIN

"Can you talk?" The text came at 6 a.m.

While I am accustomed to my former students and mentees reaching out to me, it doesn't generally happen at 6 a.m. Naturally, I felt alarmed. "Sure, what's up?" I texted back, as I tried to finish my last few reps in the weight room.

He called immediately and said, "Well, I don't know what I am doing. What's the point of all this? I was so inspired every day to train, knowing I have basketball to focus on. But now that I have graduated, nothing feels the same. I don't want to just go through life. I want to feel passion and purpose the same way I did as a high school and college athlete. How do I find that? I fear choosing the wrong path in life."

I replied with both a jab and a sad truth. "You know that quick first step you spent years looking for?" I asked. "Well, believe it or not, some people spend longer than that trying to find their calling and never do. Maybe your calling is hiding somewhere with your first step."

He laughed. Then we talked.

"The journey of blossoming into our own is complicated for all of us," I explained. "Although I can't give you exact answers about your calling, I can be transparent about my own evolution."

A JOURNEY OF MANY YEARS

I have found that genuine self-discovery often takes many years, even decades. I wasn't always an audacious, empathetic child activist, blazing trails understood mainly by fellow mavericks. Nor did I just land on Empathy Rock, shooting off ammunition in the direction of an uncaring world hurting a young person's soul.

The gift of hindsight allows me to understand that my journey into this work began long ago, not as a clinician of rescue but as a casualty of storms. The years I served facing thunderstorm after thunderstorm equipped me with the empathy needed to fight them. These days, I can easily feel the cry for help in others, as if I were the one inside of them doing the crying.

For me, this epiphany of "storm boot camp" took place in college and provided me with a defining moment. There the groundwork was laid that would lead me to genuinely care about the downpour of misfortune others would face.

What frightens us most about the tornados of life is not the calamity itself, but the uncertainty of whether things will be OK afterward. Even if you lack the exact coordinates of a journey, you can find peace in trusting that you will arrive safely at your chosen destination. When you doubt that safe outcome, however, your lack of faith brings on a rush of fear, anxiety, and hard questions.

This reality is as true for you as it is for the young people whom you influence every day. It was certainly true for my mentee on the other end of the line. I was able to share with him the time that I, too, felt lost looking for signs that my actions aligned with some purpose.

Where in your own life have you experienced such internal strife?

For a moment, imagine that you have trekked to the Gore Canyon, a Class V whitewater rapids on the Colorado River. The Colorado snakes its way over 1,450 miles, crosses between seven U.S and two Mexican states, and is known as one of the top-rated whitewater rafting locations in the world. On this adventure, consider yourself a novice rafter who has decided to dare the wild, churning waters all alone. To prepare, you bring a few tools, a primitive map, and very little guidance to help you achieve your goal. The question is never if you will complete the trek; in fact, you are sure to fail.

Imagine the thoughts running through your mind as, minutes after you begin, you sit stranded on the bank of this massive, roiling river, enveloped by the rugged mountain range and never-ending forest skyline. The only thing that outnumbers the surrounding trees are the questions ambushing your mind. The unforgiving onslaught of the whitewater rapids you just rode is eclipsed only by the rush of fear and doubt that seizes you now.

Oh, how you should have prepared better! The support you should have brought! The training you should have had! You really didn't belong here, given your physical and mental state. Fear of your uncertain future and unknown ending drive all your questions.

Have you ever found yourself in such a state? Welcome to my college years, where my soul-searching pilgrimage began.

OUT OF PLACE

In the fall of 1999, I arrived at Linfield College and discovered the little community of McMinnville, Oregon. Linfield is a small, private liberal arts school that costs more to attend than any of the region's state schools. If not for basketball, I probably never would have landed there.

Between the campus's beautiful architecture and classic small-town country feel, I certainly felt out of place. As an African American kid, my heart beat to the rhythms of my own culture's drums. The food, the slang, the music, the fashion—I was truly an urban kid. When I discovered the head coach had great energy and charisma, however, I took a liking to him.

My first year of school went by in a blur. I felt inundated by my newfound freedom, eager to establish a new normal and new relationships. Basketball went so well that at the season-ending banquet, I was named captain of the team, charged with leading the program forward.

Not until my sophomore year did this journey come to a screeching halt. This is when my true self finally started to discover and explore my core purpose.

Have you ever been in a situation where the very thing that gave you an identity was also the very thing that hindered your ability to ascend toward a breakthrough moment? For some, it's a relationship; for others, a job. For me, it was basketball. I needed basketball in my life. The sport afforded me a sense of security, but also made me wonder, *without this, what am I, really?* It's almost as though I used it to self-medicate from the trauma of foster care, watching the murder of my sister, learning of my father's death, and all the other traumatic experiences I had mentally blocked out. Basketball was my safe haven, my normal. It was the only thing I had in common with all the other kids, the one thing that allowed my life to look like theirs.

And then, that "one thing" got taken away.

My coach called me into his office one day and said, "You failed political science. You are not going to play this year."

To have basketball ripped away from me sent off stress signals throughout my body. This was my own 6 a.m. phone call that asked, "What's the point of all this?" This was my Colorado River moment. This is where I found myself shipwrecked on the side of a massive rapids with few to no past experiences to lean on, and no sure sign of hope that help was on its way.

Until I got the sign that said, "help is on its way."

My coach continued: "But you are still a part of this team. You still need to be at practice, you are still a leader on this team. This didn't just happen to you, this happened to all of us. We will get through this together."

What a scary and "feel good" moment at the same time, knowing that my coach refused to abandon me! To some degree, it helped that I would still practice every day . . . until that got taken away, as well.

During one drill, I dribbled toward the basket and went airborne to attack the rim. A teammate smashed into me high in the air. My body had no defense and I crashed to the floor, tailbone first, bracing myself with my right wrist from the dangerous fall. I suffered severe bruises to both areas and could not practice again until I healed. In textbook fashion, I expressed my frustration later by taking it out on someone who did not deserve the negative energy I gave him—a classic case of "If you don't heal what hurt you, you will bleed on people who didn't cut you."

The Black Student Union was preparing to host its annual campus-wide talent show. I was to serve that evening as the show's DJ, something that excited me. But standing in front of me that night, and frustrating my ability to do it, was a young man with long, blonde hair. Student Services had a new policy, he informed me, and they could no longer allow clubs to operate the school's sound and other equipment. We could use the equipment, he said, but he had to operate it.

His answer wasn't good enough for me that night. Not with my basketball injury, not with me being off the active roster. I argued with him, yelled at him, cursed him out—and none of it was his fault. I extended to him the emotion I should have let out, on a hill, alone, with one loud scream.

I went home that night and cried. I felt terrible that I had treated the innocent young man that way. My behavior did not reflect who I was or how my mother had raised me; and surely, if my father were still alive, I would have let him down, as well.

I bottomed out.

I'm not sure I fully recognized it at that moment, but hindsight often provides beautiful and unrivaled feelings of gratitude. That season brought about discoveries I can describe only as divine. As I continued to spiral downward, I found the anchor of my existence, which turned out to be one of the most defining moments of my life.

Today, as a career educator, I look back on the incident and understand that at that moment, I graduated from a deficiency state to a growth state, according to Maslow's Hierarchy of Needs. For the first time in my life, I began asking myself some real questions about my life calling. Those questions came to me, however, through profound sadness and doubt. I felt all alone.

If my dad was alive, I thought, *I wouldn't be at this school. He was a basketball star who was selected in the NBA draft! If I wasn't raised in a community that this culture defines as a cult, the support I would have had would look very different.* On and on it went. All the questions that one would ask out of deep desperation, I asked that night.

I frantically searched for meaning to a life scarred by group home visits and media frenzies bordering on debauchery. How could I, an innocent boy, deal with it all? I went to sleep that night with no answers and a heavy heart. The only thing colder and gloomier than that classic Oregon winter night was my emotional state. My mind reflected the grey skies, only darker and bleaker. My bed felt like a bundle of cold, damp autumn leaves, dismal to the touch.

Within hours, all of that would change.

YOU'LL GET THROUGH THIS

Legion are the stories in which some protagonist finds himself in the depths of peril, when suddenly he receives a sign that suggests, "I see you! You are going to get through this."

Has that ever happened to you? You didn't know every bend of the road ahead of you, but you felt at peace with the protection you'd just found somewhere on the ride. That's what happened to me that night.

I woke up just a few short hours after I fell asleep, but with a deep sense of calm. I'd had a dream in which I was playing basketball for Duke University. After hitting the game-winning shot, I walked off the court and found my dad standing there. In the dream, my body kind of froze in disbelief, just before I embraced my father with a big hug.

And then it was gone. I woke up the instant I hugged my dad.

What did not go away was my dad's energy, so palpable in the dream. It shouted to me, "Even though I am not here physically, I will always be with you." I couldn't sleep the rest of the night, thinking about that dream. My mind started racing.

That's when I penned one of my first poems, titled "I Had A Dream." A Jay-Z song in which he penned a poem about someone he lost heavily influenced my own theme. I had taken a poetry class that semester, thinking that it would give me a few easy credits. I also hoped it might help with my youthful yearning to meet new friends, especially of the opposite sex. I didn't realize that it would open a door to conversations I'd never had (and didn't want to have) with anyone. Poetry allowed me to verbalize, through ink on paper, the dark spots in my soul. It comforted me and helped to meet my need to be seen, even if the only onlooker was me. These poetic conversations with myself, years ago, ignited a healing process within me. If not for that practice, I wouldn't be writing this book today.

MY PEN

My pen is dedicated
To my emotions and thoughts
I found it keeps me company
When nobody can talk

I guess I shouldn't lie
I never wanted to talk
('cause my pen never judges
When my thoughts get dark)
The fear of shedding light
On thoughts too dark
A spotlight
Would cause fright
Like a dark night
In the park

So my peer group
Is adverbs, predicates, and nouns
Through my stress

Subliminals, similes, metaphors
Are found
Complex thoughts and theories,
words abound
It saves me almost daily
When my head would pound

Here's the poem I wrote that night, after my extraordinary dream about my father:

Walking off the court I went numb I said
I stopped stood still and felt dumb in the head
Cause Pops was right there he wasn't dead I said
I looked at him, he look at me and then my eyes shed
I remember hugging but that's about it I said
That's it, a friend said. That's it, I said.
Moments later that's when I awoke in my bed
Woke up kinda sober with the blues in bed
It's true, I said, never happened, never won a game for Duke I said
And Pop really is gone Pop really is dead
Well, take it as proof, she said, as proof, I said, as proof, she said
Even though you don't see him
He's always with you, she said
Excerpt from *Diary of a Poet*, "I had a dream"

After a rough night, I started to get ready for classes and decided to check my schedule. One of the first things on my list was to stop by the Multicultural Director's office. He had been bugging me for days to come by to pick up a package. After breakfast, I made my way to his office. He handed me a manila envelope.

"What is this?" I asked.

"Open it up," he replied. I tore open the top envelope, filled nearly to bursting. Some of the contents spilled onto the floor. I picked up a card from a lady who had written:

"Hello John,

My name is Stacy and I knew your father when he attended Pacific, we were classmates. I am now working at Pacific. When Barry told me you were a student at Linfield, I decided to send you this package. I want you to know your father was an amazing leader on our campus. I will never forget we were in the commons and when another female student really disrespected him, he was so mature about it, he handled it with grace. He was always that way with everyone. . . ."

The timing of this note floored me. It came right after my dream about my dad (Sign #1), and just a day after a very similar situation had happened to me, but which I had handled very poorly (Sign #2).

Then I started looking at all the other information she sent me. It felt like Christmas morning, with tons of upbeat articles about my father from his playing days. Headline after headline. I read every one a million times. My highlight was "Local hoopstar Broussard, and Bill Walton invited to the Blazers camp." I'd never seen such articles about my father. I had seen articles about my dad, more times than I can count—in the *Los Angeles Times, The Oregonian, Time* magazine. All of them had printed stories on Dad, but none of them were written in a way that would bring pride and honor to his son, me. So, to see these uplifting articles brought gladness to my heart in a way I'd never felt.

It didn't dawn on me for a good five or ten minutes, but what I discovered next would lead me to never again question my journey (Sign #3). This discovery would ignite my purpose and give me my sole focus. As I scanned one image of my father, getting a shot off in flight over a defender, I noticed he wore number 30. I stood in awe, recognizing that the first time I picked up a jersey in middle school basketball, my number was 30. On every team I had played with since, it was the same. I fought for that number my whole playing career, but only as a superstitious athlete angling for every advantage I could get. I never knew my father also had worn number 30.

The revelational magnitude of that moment did not escape me. From the dream, to the handwritten note, to the jersey number discovery, all within eight hours of each other—I cried again. But this time, I wept tears of joy. I was able to look up to the skies and say, "You do see me! I do matter!"

From that moment, my whole life would be defined by a phrase: "Walk by faith, not by sight 30/30." Believing in things unseen gave me a determined hope that my past was only grooming me for my future. As unsure as I felt about what that future might hold, I still found the power to put to rest the aching feeling that my future was not meant to be as bright or as magnificent as that of my peers. My life changed at that moment. I was now ready to fulfill the purpose for which I had been created. At that instant, the chains of my pain fell off and destiny became visible.

MASLOW'S THEORY IN REAL LIFE

When you are forced to survive, you are not allowed to dream. That sad fact about a struggling soul escapes most of us. Growth happens only after a sense of calm comes over us. Once we know that things are not as dire as we imagined, we liberate ourselves and foster the ability to learn and grow from our life situation. We move past survival questions and start asking self-actualization questions. That's when we start to make new discoveries.

If you have devoted yourself to working with young people or are engaged with anyone in the process of self-discovery who, so far, has failed to find personal direction, I strongly urge you to ponder Maslow's theory of a "hierarchy of needs."

Abraham Maslow was an American psychologist born in 1908, best known for creating his theory of psychological health predicated on fulfilling human needs in sequential order. Maslow suggested that before someone could ask questions centered around purpose (or as he coined it, "self-actualization"), they first must have certain needs met. Stage 1, for example, is called physiological needs, the necessity of things such as food, water, and rest. Once those basics have been secured, the needs at Stage 2, "safety needs," can be met. Maslow's theory posits a total of five stages, with the last one, "self-actualization," geared toward achieving one's full potential.

Maslow published his widely accepted theory in 1943, and although in 1987 he clarified that a "need" does not have to be completely met before someone can move on to the next stage, it is difficult for one to reach the last stages of human needs without first meeting the initial stages.

On your journey to discover passion and purpose, where is this moment highlighted in your life? Moreover, do you recognize these stages in the lives of those you are trying to influence? So often as leaders, mentors, coaches, and educators, we ask subjects to achieve success at stages that lie beyond them. They are not ready for Stages 4 and 5 if they still lack the ability to move beyond Stage 2.

In my own life, I've identified a crucial Maslow moment during my sophomore year in college. What I learned that year allowed me to go from stage 4 to 5, with zero reservations, for the first time in my life. I was in full search for a purpose, the lack of which had turned my past so dark. At that moment, I found passion, fire, and desire. I found that the very thing that fatigued the life out of me also fueled me to wake up at 4 a.m. and do it all over again. And isn't that the point of it all?

As the rest of my journey unfolds, you will see how the twists and turns of my ability to fulfill my destiny has only confirmed that my past was not happenstance. My darkest nights are now being used as the brightest lights for the young people I serve—and I wouldn't trade it for the world.

"THIS WORK WAS MEANT FOR ME"

As I unfold some of the battles I have faced standing on the front lines of child liberation, my only hope is that this journey resonates with you in a way that brings conviction about your own destined path. I hope you find confirmation for your search in the same way my mentee found confirmation for his search when we spoke that morning on the phone. While reading on may not provide you with your exact landing spot of purpose, I hope to point you in the right direction until your soul stops and says, "I am here. This is home. This work was meant for me."

I encourage you to find key times to stop reading. Put the book down and reflect on what you have encountered. Such self-discovery will aid your desire to influence change and birth hope in all those you serve. Seeing yourself accurately will help you to see your students fully, and in that way, you will find the strength to care for them deeply.

2

THE INVISIBLE CHILD

Our past shapes our future whether we realize it or not.
Remembering well is as important as doing well.

JONITA MULLINS

At the tail end of 2018, on the Friday before school ended for Christmas break, I attended a staff Christmas party to enjoy the awkward company of colleagues socializing in non-work settings. You know, the parties where everyone acts nice. You love your work life, but the company celebrations always remind you that the laughs you share from 9-5 differ substantially from the diversity you enjoy in your "normal" social environment. It had that type of vibe.

In the middle rounds of holiday cheer, disguised as a White Elephant gift exchange, I received a text message from a student I mentor.

"Mr. Broussard, we may need a ride."

Considering it was after 10 p.m., I knew things must have been dire. What unfolded over the course of the next few weeks would break my heart, as though once again I were trapped in the early '90s, trying to navigate a world I could not control. As if I were once again a young, observant boy sitting in a corner, with his hands wrapped around his knees for extra protection, as a circus of mayhem swirled around me.

It's quite the paradox, my career.

THE BEGINNING OF EMPATHY

If you work with young people, it should be a job requirement that you can identify emotional spaces in yourself that look identical to those of the audience you want to influence. Real empathy begins, I think, when you know who you are and where you have been emotionally. Identifying that emotion in yourself will allow you to identify that same emotion in others.

The artist Jay-Z took a saying from the black community and inserted it into one of his songs: "I put my hand over my heart, that means I feel you, 'Real recognize Real' and you lookin' familiar." It basically means that because I am familiar with my own characteristics or situation, I can recognize the same skill set or dilemma when I see it in others. That line, although trendy, is truly the underpinning of genuine empathy—and it's on full display in the middle of a major hip hop album. If I could apply that same philosophy to our line of work, the saying might go, "real emotion recognizes real emotion," or "real distress recognizes real distress." I intentionally and repeatedly put myself in those positions.

My emotions often feel like those of a time traveler, constantly getting thrown in and out of various situations as I fight to save the lives of young people in real time. As they endure onslaughts of unexpected and unwelcome trials, I relive the period in my own life when I first started gathering the tools needed to offer support to students in their time of distress. In this case, with the student who needed a ride at 10 p.m. over Christmas break, I channeled a time in my life I call "invisible me."

A HEART INSTANTLY HEAVY

As soon as the first newspaper landed on my desk, a familiar jolt of anxiety swept over me. My heart instantly grew heavy. It felt as though I hurt physically for the two young men whose world suddenly got turned upside down by what appeared to be the feature story for every student publication and professional news media outlet in sight.

It all started with an email notifying staff members that a parent of two of our students had been arrested on the side of the road as she returned home from a school event. The authorities had been trailing her, and now she was being held for the alleged murder of a celebrity. Our students, we were told, would likely feel emotionally distraught.

Over the next few weeks, I witnessed the bedlam surrounding these innocent, amazingly strong young men. I was reminded that, in the hands of society, intrusion and invasion offer levels of stress and discomfort that no young person should ever experience, especially when those circumstances are uncontrollable. These boys had to endure the public scrutiny of their family's misfortunes on TMZ, Dateline, and other local and national media outlets.

To make matters worse, they then had to walk a large school campus, daily being reminded that their world was not normal. The strained body language of students and teachers alike, the timid "hellos," and the awkward "How are yous" all reminded me that this is not normal treatment for the average emotionally stable child.

The unusual circumstances of these two students provided evidence to me that while we can try to run from our past, divinity has a way of utilizing that past to provide aid to the hurting as well as discernment for the future.

DISGUISED AND HIDING

Prior to college, I spent my early to late teen years in hiding. I did everything I could to be normal emotionally, physically, and socially.

I wanted to disguise myself from the very thing, my past, that today lights my soul on fire.

I spent much of my pre-teen years feeling like a zoo animal, present to the world only to feed its insatiable curiosity about the strange or the weird. My idea of normal was to be a circus attraction. I felt stuck, center stage, in a crowded tent, frozen in place until the last spectator moved on to the next freak show.

I had a strong desire to remain hidden at all costs, to stay invisible in the crowd. In pre-college, therefore, I camouflaged myself so that I could disappear on campus. I crowd-surfed different peer groups, but never dipped so deep in the water as to truly be seen. The basketball team, the track team—it didn't matter. I picked up friends everywhere and absorbed their "normal" as if it were my own . . . and in some fashion, it really was. I enjoyed adolescent amusements and welcomed as many of them as I could lay my hands on. I thought of them as extra layers of protection, as my invisibility cloak.

Underneath my disguise, however, lay my irreplaceable core—the same core that today identifies with my students. My experience tells me that remaining close to your emotional center allows the flame of empathy to spark and burn in your soul.

I knew the heart of my two students caught in the glare of lurid news headlines, because I knew my own. Most often, I prefer not to be reminded of my past, so in this case, I didn't remind them, either. Think of a physical mark left on your body—students do not like walking a campus where they are repeatedly reminded that they have a deformed or missing limb. You are missing a leg, you are missing an arm, you are missing a normal childhood. It's all the same. Condolences, therefore, can feel like confirmation. They remind us that things are very wrong.

All of us want to *feel* normal, even if we know we cannot *be* normal. I knew deep inside however, that eventually I would leave my campus façade behind and return to a home that triggered reminders of everything but normal. That parts of my upbringing would challenge society's definition of an extended family. I would not see my dad there. I might see my deceased sister, but only in random flashbacks that felt more like flash bangs. I knew my invisible was only pretend, and that the campus where I walked daily knew it, too; but that was OK by me.

> *I really can't relate*
> *To third world blues*
> *Never have walked*
> *In third world shoes*
> *But I really can feel*
> *They bad news*
>
> *I know what it's like*
> *2 lose a dad too*
>
> *I also came from a shelter*
> *That was helter skelter*
> *All alone in the world*
> *Where no one would help a*
> *Poor little boy*
> *Who was all alone*

Excerpt from *Diary of a Poet,* "Third World Blues"

Navigating my position as Athletic Director to protect these young men from a barrage of media requests, all of those feelings returned—only now the complexity of my emotions poured out as if it were all happening to *me*, yet again. I was protecting them, but it felt as if I were also protecting myself.

My spirit at that time exuded energies of "just go away." At the direction of the boys' family, I was happy to deliver that message to one particularly intrusive national media outlet: "Just go away." When I received calls about doing "interest pieces" on the boys, I was content to say, "just go away." My advice to my colleagues was simple: act normal. The last thing these boys needed was a campus of 2,800 people, all serving as Doctor Phil. They did not need us to be him or any other advisory phycologist.

These amazing boys had the gift of taking center stage and did so often; but this was one performance no child should ever have to give. Normal, invisible, supportive, was far better. This I knew. This I felt.

LIFE COMES FULL CIRCLE

Life has a way of coming full circle when you refuse to shut out emotionally-charged experiences from the past. My family also has gone through times of unbearable scrutiny, such as when my dad appeared in 1988 on the nationally televised *Oprah Winfrey Show* to talk about the beating death of my sister, Dayna. I know well the media circus that often follows such a tragedy. My heightened awareness of the excruciating emotions I felt back then allowed me to have a high level of empathy for these young men, almost as if I were literally walking in their shoes at that moment.

Each day when one of these young men would escape campus life to hang out in my office, the environment remained the same as it had been prior to their time of grief. We joked some days; we talked some days; some days we didn't talk at all. I worked and they sat quietly. Mentally and emotionally, it was as if I served three purposes at once:

- I was helping these young men find some control over an out-of-control world.

- I was reliving a moment for the "invisible" young boy who still breathes inside of me.
- I was the adult shielding both innocent boys from a world looking to highlight just how abnormal, unfair, and cruel life can be.

Remaining empathetic toward the wounded students I serve may feel as natural for me as you giving a history lecture that you have spent your tenth year covering, or as a veteran coach describing his patented, championship-winning man-to-man defense. The truth is, on every campus, walking every hallway, sitting in every classroom, exists a child whose emotional distress needs to be acknowledged and spoken for. They are begging to be seen but not prodded.

How, though, can we do that? And what's the difference between "seen" and "prodded"?

SYMPATHY VS. EMPATHY

When trauma hits our youth, most educators employ the emotional tool called sympathy, even though it's empathy that really changes things. Empathy requires you to really see the child, to perceive the child as if that child were you. Failing to really see the child thwarts any attempt at effectively activating empathy.

Empathy is what the two students on my campus needed. It's what I needed as a child. And the call for empathy is the plaintive cry of hundreds of thousands of unseen children trudging across school campuses all around the country. We feel the sympathy, but we need the empathy. Do we understand the difference?

Webster's dictionary describes empathy as "the understanding and sharing of the emotions and experiences of another person." Wikipedia offers a more expanded definition that fosters a clearer understanding: "Empathy is the capacity to understand or feel what another person is experiencing from within their frame of reference, that is, the capacity to place oneself in another's position. Definitions of empathy encompass a broad range of emotional states." This second definition underscores the power of empathy to help educators relate more effectively to young people.

By contrast, note how Webster defines sympathy: "sorrow or pity for another." Wikipedia defines sympathy as "the perception, understanding, and reaction to the distress or need of another life form." While showing sympathy can be good, sympathy is no substitute for empathy.

How well do we grasp the vast difference between sympathy and empathy? Can we appreciate the critical distinction between the two? Empathy requires a dialed-in emotional connection with ourselves, along with our students, in order to recognize another's pain as our own. The real game changer comes when we recognize another's misfortune as our misfortune. That's the miracle ingredient—not just feeling bad about someone's terrible plight.

I admit that I don't always empathize with my students. Sometimes, I don't slow down enough to really place myself emotionally in their shoes. We're all humans; at times, we all fall short. Even so, I absolutely recognize that my greatest success stories in impacting young lives always connect to my understanding the child, seeing the child, and responding as if I were the one emotionally tight-roping each shaky step across campus.

As a staff, I believe we effectively handled the delicacy of the boys' situation. We all recognized their anguish, even as the boys themselves did. We managed to create a shield for them transparent enough to allow their "normal" to exist despite the off-campus circus. Maybe a teacher gave the boys a simple extension on an assignment, allowing them to turn in their work a little late so they could avoid campus traffic during passing period. Or maybe they had a long, quiet lunch with me—subtle things that acknowledged our awareness and care without alarming the boys or drawing attention to their abnormal reality. Some days they expressed a need to be seen a little more than others, but most days they remained mostly invisible. As a campus, we were ready for both. We did our best to fully "see" both young men.

TACTFULLY TEACHING

We educators often miss altogether the most critical element of school success. In our enthusiastic pursuit of transforming a student's mind from position A to position Z, too often we forget the emotional development needed to reach the former objective. And when this happens, any performance progress we might hope to gain begins to cough, stall, and die.

Have you ever experienced an educator who failed to recognize that teaching a subject also involves teaching people born with feelings? Part of the teaching process means communicating with care. We do not want to resemble the physician bereft of a good bedside manner. He walks in, tells you have stage 4 cancer, and then asks if you watched the big game last night. He leaves you wondering, How did that man get this job? Emotionally inept educators should be in an office writing curriculum, not on the front lines of classrooms filled with students or on the baselines of basketball courts running practice.

Most coaches and educators who sign up for the work of shepherding young minds into healthier spaces also possess a toolbox filled with helpful instruments designed to increase their own emotional intelligence. For the trauma-filled child, what separates progression from depression is an educator sharpening those tools and becoming an expert. In the workbook, we'll take a closer look at these tools, but the most common practices for empathy include:

- Having a genuine curiosity about your students' lives
- Releasing preconceived notions about your students—don't assume you know why they act or perform as they do
- Trying to imagine how you would face the stresses they face
- Understanding that vulnerability goes both ways
- Remaining sensitive toward views and opinions that differ from your own.

The workbook also will help you to take a deeper look into your own emotional journey. What experiences in your life can you harness to identify the many emotions your students face on campus? How can you use every single emotion, wasting nothing? The more equipped you are at seeing yourself emotionally, the better chance you will have at seeing your students empathetically.

How would you evaluate the state of your own empathy toolbox? The tools described above include only the most common ones; unusual trauma often calls for specialized tools. Do you have any of those specialized tools in your toolbox? If not, do you know where and how to acquire them?

As we press forward in this book, I will continue to press forward into you, and especially into your heart. I will attempt to draw into you in ways that I hope will allow you to better draw into your students, so that you can see them in the way they so desperately need to be seen.

Most of that "drawing in" starts with you knowing all the parts of you that store your past emotional experiences, including the good, the bad, and the frightening. Even the embarrassing ones! I recall the time I shanked three dunks off the rim in front of a large college audience. I wanted to run and hide as the liquid courage that had filled the crowd with confidence also enticed them to laugh. Very loudly. At me.

I never wanted to relive that moment, until one of my mentees called me twenty years later after leaving a dunk contest held in front of a noisy crowd. His legs felt "off," he told me, so the ball kept bouncing off the rim. I laughed and said, "Let me tell you a story." Eventually we laughed together, and his distress ebbed away. That is what emotional empathy looks like.

Get in touch with all the varying emotions you have felt over your lifetime, and why you felt them. You never know when you will need to retrieve a certain emotional experience! That moment will suddenly appear, like a pop quiz. When? None of us knows, but I assure you it will pop up. Are you ready?

USE YOUR PAST TO ENHANCE THEIR FUTURE

I am a firm believer that a past not used to enhance the world around you is useless. Our experiences serve only as combustible energy, allowing our emotions to evolve into the specific passion that points us toward the path we were called to walk, even from infancy.

In this book, I use my experiences as examples to suggest how our quest forward always aligns with our previous paths. Even before taking my first step, my destiny was determined. Every part of my journey has been used to enhance and energize my steps forward. Yours can serve the same purpose.

If you dig deep enough, you will find how life's twists and turns have shaped your own heart to beat to the rhythms of steps you already have taken—the gallops as well as the stumbles. Every step you take serves a vital role. Every step is a tool you need for the here and now.

No step is ever wasted. We can ignore our missteps, but if you are truly committed to working with young people, I challenge you to refuse to ignore any of your past experiences. Dig deep inside. Find the "why" behind every layer of purpose. And grab hold of its confirming destiny in your life, both for your personal benefit and for the benefit of the young people you serve.

TIME FOR SELF-ASSESSMENT

How do you rate your ability to empathize and meet young people where they are emotionally? I'd guess that most of us imagine we have earned a much greater score than we deserve, because we all want to play the role of hero to a young person in urgent need of wellness. We might not be aware that we can sharpen our tools in certain areas.

When did you last do an honest assessment of the impact you have on your students? What intentional habits are you creating to ensure you are properly equipped? Are your current methods working? Would your students or players agree with you?

Now is a perfect time to put down this book and ask yourself some hard questions. Ask your colleagues, too. And don't forget to ask your students (and not only the ones who gravitate toward you).

If you want to grow personally through the remaining chapters, don't skip an honest personal assessment. We all have blind spots, me included. What are yours?

3

NAVIGATING TRAGEDY

Feelings buried alive never die.

KAROL K. TRUMAN

In the autumn of 2012, our nation sat down in front of overflowing plates of love disguised as sweet potato pie, turkey, and mashed potatoes. The aroma of Thanksgiving seduces even the most independent of hearts, beckoning them home.

Where is that place for you? What smells do you inhale and what tales would you tell to describe Thanksgiving? Perhaps football with the guys, while mom cooks the feast. Maybe you picture sitting around the living room in pajamas, while the family watches the big parade on TV. Whatever euphoria you experience, I want you to picture that joy turned to pain. That love turned to loss. If it weren't for the massive knots in your stomach, your belly would be empty altogether. The idea of holding down *any* food, let alone holiday cheer, would produce a sickening feeling throughout your whole body.

Welcome to Thanksgiving week, 2012. Especially November 17. The day Dylan passed.

TONGUE TWISTED

Trying to extract significance from senselessness is like trying to grab a handful of air to describe its texture. Or to change the image, you have this inner belief that some substance exists in the soil, but you can't get to it because it's buried somewhere beneath the sadness. Unearthing it seems overwhelming.

If you listen closely, however, you can hear a quiet voice saying, "a great commission will be birthed out of this devastation." But trying to describe, define, or pinpoint exactly why certain things happen? Well, that task is clearly impossible. In fact, it can leave your conscious mind contorted. I felt exactly like that the day I found myself trying to comfort a thousand grieving hearts in a packed gym as we celebrated the life of one of the greatest souls I've ever known.

Dylan's death hit me hard. In a sad, detached kind of way, his death hit me harder even than the passing of certain beloved family members. A numbness always comes over me with someone's death. It's my way of coping, I guess (or not coping at all, now that I think about it). I suppose I am a casualty of war.

For me, loss became normalized at an age when I longed for understanding but received instead a dark legacy recounted by soldiers. For warriors encamped in a place saturated with the smell of death, grieving a death takes a back seat to winning the war. I learned that the most pressing goal is simply to get home safe.

For others, home was a vision, a place to return to. For me, home was a prayer, a place I hoped to find someday. Life had robbed me of a healthy grieving process. It stole from me healthy examples of empathy.

Yet here I stood, at thirty-one years of age, being asked to empathize a great loss for myself and others in my school community. Strangely, this felt like the first time in my life I had to do this. *It's the first time I've lost a loved one when a war didn't rage around me,* I realized. This time, the war was *in* me.

I didn't do this part of empathy particularly well. Something inside me preferred the other kind of war, the one I knew. It can be powerful, though, to recognize your deficits in empathy, because with intentional work on the inside, you can foster a life fully lived on the outside—a complete life. I recognized my empathy deficit, and although I struggled, I welcomed the battle of making peace within myself while trying to provide peace for others.

In the previous chapter, I focused on knowing ourselves. In this chapter, I emphasize knowing others. How do we improve our ability to communicate and decipher someone else's emotions, and then paint the picture so clearly that it deeply resonates with people?

Which brings me to an epiphany.

GRIEVING WITH GOD AND OTHERS

I think black communities should learn to grieve with each other the same way we have learned to grieve with God. If we learned to express to each other the agonies we express to God, just maybe our communities would heal better. Heal together. Maybe then I could have healed better. Maybe if the right questions had been asked of me, I would now have the right answers for others—a thought, I guess, I should express to God.

I went to God a lot when Dylan passed, and not just for me, but also for a school community of grievers who stood with me as we all supported his devastated family. Since I knew that life experiences trigger each individual in a unique way, I genuinely wanted to bring unity. I wanted to honor Dylan and his life in a way that his experience would speak to the lives of the thousand-plus individuals in the gym that day. I wanted to speak to each griever as an individual, as though Dylan's story were *their* story.

That's what empathy is, right? Instead of Dylan's family being in the front row to my right, it was your family. Instead of Dylan's teammates and coaches sitting in the front row to my left, it was your teammates and coaches. I knew that some of those in the room did not know Dylan well. They had come to support their own child or a colleague. Maybe they felt numb to Dylan's loss, like losses I've faced. I really didn't know the proper way to empathize with so many individuals at one time. I was just entering a point in my life where, for the first time, I had begun grieving for myself.

I discovered, however, that by grieving Dylan's death in a healthy way—by recapturing who he was and highlighting our amazing time together—for the first time in my life, my grief for Dylan released emotions I had about my sister that had remained buried since the day I watched her die in front of me. While I am not sure this felt "good," I do recognize it as both healthy and healing.

The day after the ceremony, the father of a set of twin boys I taught emailed me a story that echoed this tragic incident. He didn't know Dylan well, but spoke of a childhood friend who had passed. Attending Dylan's service, he said, brought back memories and healing he did not know that he needed, even thirty years later. I learned from this experience that, like storms, the seasons we face often require cleanup. The lightning comes and goes, the thunder roars and passes, and in time, the night gives way to day. Mother Nature and Father Time will come with a surety, and when they do, it becomes vital for our wellness that we do our part by acknowledging the damage caused and that we commit to cleaning things up on the inside. For me, that cleanup started by acknowledging the experience I had with both Dylan and my sister Dayna.

HIS TIME TO SHINE

Dylan and I had been on a journey. He represented the spirit of all teenage boys peeking into manhood, like the sun breaking through clouds in the morning sky. His time to shine had dawned upon us all. He had visions of greatness about achievement, but also doubt. What made Dylan incredibly rare is that at a young age, up until the time he passed at age sixteen, he possessed an unquenchable thirst for his passion, along with an obsession for a strong work ethic. He radiated delight and enhanced every environment he entered.

Dylan was the perfect temperature on a spring day. He was your rainbow after the rain. He was the vision of educators on the first day of school, dreaming about how great the year would be. I poured my heart into him and together we stared destiny in the face. Like a great movie, I felt riveted to each scene of his life, on the edge of my seat anticipating the next moment, knowing it would be more glorious than any before. That is how everyone felt about Dylan.

The bond I shared with him, he shared with so many. He was just that type of kid. He had everyone glued to their seat, emotionally transfixed, rooting him on every day. That was our normal.

Until it wasn't. Without warning, it all stopped. The cheers, the smiles, his joy, our joy, our hearts. His heart. It *all* stopped.

Has that happened to you? Chances are, if you are a veteran educator, you have experienced the loss of a young person. I didn't know how to cope with Dylan's passing. I struggled immensely with its finality.

How could I just erase the dreams we shared? How could I dream a new dream when he played the starring role? How could I help a room full of people find purpose in devastation? Like a dark cloud racing over a blue sky, an onslaught of painful flashbacks hit me. A lightning bolt of emotion flashed through my mind and the anxiety of the moment pierced every nerve in my body. I was rendered helpless, numb, confused, lost. I turned inward, embracing the seven-year-old boy who still sat on a cold garage floor, watching his sister get beaten to death.

Madeleine L'Engle said, "the great thing about getting older is that you don't lose all the other ages you've been." In that moment, I was no longer the thirty-one-year-old man grieving the death of Dylan. I was the seven-year-old boy finding closure and insight from the death of his sister, Dayna. There's always an enlightening component involved in our healing process, a moment that not only defines where you have been, but also that shines light on where you are headed.

GROUND ZERO

For better or worse, who I've been has served as the underpinning of who I am today. And Dayna's death proved to be the epicenter of it all. Her lifeless body became my ground zero.

At seven years of age, I was too young to find significance in numbers, and yet at the same time, I was old enough to wear memories like tattoos. No amount of scrubbing can erase the scars. No number of years can dissipate the heavy feeling that sticks to my skin like moisture.

On that cold garage floor in October of 1988, dreams and aspirations still lie. My sister's future is suspended in time, holding on to tomorrow like the tight grip of her oppressors' hands grasping the "hose and other torture instruments" used to tear skin from her precious nine-year-old body. The *L.A. Times* reported my sister was struck as many as 800 times. (*Los Angeles Times, October 21st, 1988*), I've read other articles that claim the number was closer to 200. No one will ever know the exact number. The brutality of it remains more significant than any number ever could.

During an appearance on the *Oprah Winfrey* show, my father acknowledged the tragic situation but also described the discipline handed out as "spankings." He went on to say, "In Watts, parents have seen brutality that would trip the mind of the average American" (Oprah Winfrey Show, October 20, 1988). I was far too young to understand the violence that plagued the community of Watts, California, during the '80s, but all that changed after one dreadful evening. I am certain the brutality in Watts was not a qualifying remark to place perspective on the violence unleashed upon my sister; but then and even now, violence is still violence and innocence is still innocence. In that moment, I was exposed to the former and stripped of the latter.

It doesn't even haunt me, to be honest, the precise number of strikes it took to take Dayna's life. Nor am I conflicted that the four adults accused of her murder found it sane to hang a nine-year-old child out of a window by her stomach immediately after their lethal flogging. What does absorb my thoughts are my sister's aspirations. In that moment, instead of being forced to count the number of lashings delivered, I wish instead I could have counted the number of dreams she had. What she hoped for, what goals she had in life. I wish I could have counted her desires. Those are the thoughts that linger.

I kinda wish now
Way back when
When we still spoke
I would have asked you then
If you could see 20
What you would have been

Think about it
Can you picture it yet
Can you picture the little girl
In the window set
  Come on
  Think about it
  Can you picture it yet
  Can you picture the little girl
  In the window set

It really don't make sense to me
What's the point or purpose
of your history?
When all it really was
Was misery
Excerpt from *Diary of Poet,* "Think about it, can you picture it yet?"

Something about the death of a young person haunts your soul. It's not the number of days they lived that rots your stomach, but the number of days taken away. It feels incomplete. It feels like watching an amazing movie that has completely drawn you in and then, with no warning, ends right before the climax. It leaves you unsettled and restless, constantly wondering about the "what ifs."

When a person of mature age passes, our focus changes. The moment of remembrance gets engulfed in recognition of a life fully lived. It is easier to find peace with that perspective.

But with the untimely death of a young person, a part of you stirs forever. Trying to find that peace and purpose, however, is the only thing that allows you to truly move forward. It's where I found myself emotionally trying to rationalize the loss of Dylan.

FINDING PEACE THROUGH TRAGEDY

I searched for the right words not only to comfort, but also to convict, a community of grieving spirits to breathe still. Achieve still. Ascend still. Without warning, that is when my subconscious took me back through my own journey to find the tools I used to keep going.

In the moments I dealt with the pain of losing Dylan, I found hope through the peace I'd gained in dealing with the tragedy of losing my sister. Although I had never experienced anything like trying to recognize and speak to the hearts of others, in some ways I was able, by going through that process of empathy, to connect to the grieving hearts of an entire school community. I felt prepared for the moment.

As an influencer of young people, the greatest strength you possess is not your skill but your ability to recognize the heart of others. To maximize both, you must maximize yourself. Part of that equation is human experience. You must hold dear the moments in your life where you felt the same degree of emotion as that of the ones you lead. The depths you will go to bring healing when healing is required depends on your ability to imagine that level of loss–or better yet, to have literally gone through similar loss yourself. The effectiveness of your leadership depends on your ability to communicate, "Where you are now, I once was."

Belief births hope, and it's that hope that allows the brokenhearted to begin the journey of healing. Healed not because the loss becomes less significant, but because in front of the griever stands a person who carried the same afflictions, and yet who found a way to be freed from the bondage of life's tragedies.

FINDING MY VOICE

Although it took me days to navigate the appropriate convictions my spirit wished to convey, eventually I found myself and my voice. So, there I stood, on November 22, 2012, in an overflowing gymnasium. I looked over the crowd. The atmosphere reeked of despair. In a place typically filled with jubilant noise, today it remained deafeningly quiet. It was as if the star basketball player that had captivated both home and away spectators had suddenly dropped dead in the middle of competition.

Well, that's almost exactly what had happened. Dylan was our star. He had passed away in his sleep from complications with his heart. Directly in front of me and to the right sat his mother, Lisa; father, Joe; his brother, CJ; and sister, Daniele, who we called Danny. It still hurts my soul, picturing the level of pain on their faces, on everyone's face. In the middle of this quiet storm, the room's posture screamed, "Help me!"

It took a few awkward moments for words to exit my mouth. The first few times I tried to speak, nothing came out, regardless of how hard I tried. My mouth felt both warm and watery and yet dry at the same time. My stomach felt queasy, as if I were going to lose my lunch all over the microphone. I took a step back to gather myself. Preparing for this moment, I had one goal. I wanted to honor my student, my player, my friend. I prayed for strength, and with determined sadness, I told the Dylan Weinmann story.

REMEMBERING DYLAN

I had my last workout with Dylan a few days before he passed. It was 5:30 a.m. Friday and I hadn't seen him yet. It was still dark outside and only a few people had shown up at the gym.

I leaned up off the weight bench and texted Dylan, "Where are you?"

I wasn't quite sure he would text back because he always forgot his phone, something his mother and I often grumbled about. To my surprise, he actually had it on him that morning. "in gym," his text said.

I left the weight room and headed to the gym. I stood there and watched for a minute, like I'd done so many other mornings. Just one kid in a gym, chasing his dream. Eventually, I opened the door when I noticed him lethargically shooting a floater with his left hand.

"What was *that*?" I asked him. "That's not a game shot. Be explosive! Attack the rim! You have to go game speed now in order to get better in the game."

"Whatever," he answered, then added sarcastically, "I was up late doing homework."

"Tell that excuse to your college coach," I replied, and walked out the door. I knew that was all he needed to hear.

When I walked by ten minutes later, he was starting his drill at half court. At full speed, he dribbled behind his back in one direction. One handed crossover in another direction, a spin move, and ended it with a floater with his left hand. If you ever saw Dylan dribble a ball, you'd know what I'm describing. His movements were so fluid, like poetry. Just smooth.

I finished my own workout about 6:30 a.m., so I headed over to work with Dylan one-on-one for the last half hour, a routine we'd been doing since his basketball season ended the previous year.

My role is almost like a trainer for a boxer, probably 80 percent mental and 20 percent physical. "What's the difference between you and the best shooter in the world?" I asked.

"Practice and repetition," he replied. And he shot another set of twenty jump shots.

"Who's the best shooter you know?"

"I am," he answered with confidence. And he shot another set of twenty jump shots.

"What's going to make you get up at 5 a.m., even when the season starts, just to come to the gym?"

"Because I want to be the best." And he shot another set of twenty jump shots.

I've been in education since 2003, and as a teacher/coach/mentor, I'm not supposed to have favorites. So, for that reason, I won't say Dylan was mine. But to understand how Dylan got to this point for me, I would have to start back at my first year at Linfield Christian Private School five years before, when Dylan as a sixth grader showed up to basketball tryouts.

I had organized a drill in which the boys lined up at the baseline. They had to dribble down the court, cross over in front, come back down the court, and cross over behind the back. As I looked at the thirty-plus boys, I had one of those moments when, as a coach, you think, *We're not winning a game this year.*

Then I saw Dylan, the smallest guy on the court, just elbows and kneecaps. He was dribbling down with his head up, no stumbles, just confidence. Over at the layup drill, he went up with both his left and right hand, perfectly. By the end of tryouts, I picked Dylan and eleven other boys to play with him. We ended up going undefeated that year.

That's when I knew Dylan was a special kid.

If you knew Dylan as well as I did, you knew he had the same questions every young boy has:

Can I reach my dream?

Do I have what it takes?

Am I heroic?

No one in life wants to fail. Little kids don't grow up thinking, I *don't want to reach my dreams.* They never say, "I don't want to live a life of passion" or "I don't want to be dedicated."

But somehow, life on this earth has a way of stripping our hope from us, making us feel the task is too great or that we're not strong enough/fast enough/brilliant enough to reach our goals. I see that look on the faces of the students I work with. I see that on the faces of adults I'm around.

Dylan was not that way. He was firmly resolved to see his dream come true—and that was Dylan's greatest strength: his dedication to keep improving. He knew it wouldn't come easy, but by God Almighty, it would come.

That same dedication would have made him successful in anything. That dedication crosses all facets of life. It just so happens that Dylan loved basketball.

And boy, was he dedicated.

When I met him, he could dribble but he couldn't shoot a pebble into a pond standing on a boat. That was also his insecurity; but slowly, surely, year after year, he got better. After school, before school, at 7 a.m. in the summertime, he continued to work on his shot as I continued to work on his confidence. Somewhere between those workouts, when I was trying to give him confidence, he ended up taking my heart.

A question I always have is not how individuals become great, but what makes them want to become great. What makes them do abnormal things to stand out above the rest? I can give a player a workout plan all day long, but what I can't give a kid is the desire, hunger, and dedication to be the best. That comes only from within.

Dylan figured that out. On his last day on earth, Dylan was zoned in. Nothing and no one would stop his dream from becoming a reality.

As he attempted shot after shot in the gym that day and I asked him to name the best shooter he knew, his answer didn't come from a boastful place. It came from confidence; he knew sacrifice would help him to become great. He knew that with each shot he took, his dream got one step closer to becoming real. That's why Dylan was great.

With the great ones, we don't simply mourn their death; we celebrate their life.

There's no sense in trying to find answers to what happened to Dylan. Like many other questions in life, those are reserved for the Most High. If Dylan meant anything to us, we simply honor him. I, along with his other coaches, mentors, and educators, we honor him.

A few days ago, I spoke about Dylan with Bruce Scheibe, who coached alongside me. "There will never be another Dylan," I said. "But the reality is, we honor Dylan's life by making sure there is another Dylan. We continue to inspire the next Dylan. We must find the next Dylans and pour confidence into them. They must come to believe what we were able help Dylan believe, that 'he who is in you is greater than he who is in the world,' and 'all things are possible for those who believe in Christ.'"

On the day I gave my tribute to Dylan, I also gave several challenges to those in the audience. I knew Dylan's memory had to be more than just a celebration of life. It also had to be a commission of how to live ours.

"Teammates of Dylan," I said, "honor him. When you're at practice, when you're tired, when you're at home playing video games or social networking . . . think of Dylan. Honor him by changing your work ethic, thus pushing you to become the best player possible.

"Dylan's classmates and friends, honor him. This is not a basketball story, but simply a story of a boy who had a dream. You could be the next doctor, the next drama star, whatever it is. Have the dedication to perfect your craft. That's how you honor him.

"Dylan's family, you honor Dylan by your strength. Dylan was the strongest kid I know, something he learned from you. Tough times do not last, but tough families do.

"*That's* how we honor Dylan. As we gather to say goodbye to Dylan's earthly shell, we remember that his spirit lives forever. His spirit lives forever in my heart, as well as in all those he touched. Let's honor him forever by the way we continue to live. . . ."

WHAT LOSS HAVE YOU ENDURED?

Dylan's memorial service was, by far, the toughest moment in my career. I understand that not every educator has had to face tragedy at such an intense level, especially those still in the infancy stages of their career. The longer you remain in education, however, the devastation of loss becomes inevitable. It seems to impact my school environment every year.

Has that happened to you? Has your classroom or practice setting been affected by the unthinkable? If not by death, possibly by another tragedy? What was it, and how did you handle it?

None of us is ever quite ready for these moments, for two reasons. First, we're not trained to be ready for them. Second, we never receive warning when such a climate shift will strike.

Pressing forward through tragedy is a delicate space to navigate. Meeting the diverse needs of a grieving campus can send your heart into palpitations. Act normal, or act broken? Change routine, or business as usual? I have been both the griever and reliever, and I can attest that it starts with knowing the heart of your audience. What are they feeling and why? The answers to those questions are buried in your ability to employ empathy. Those answers are key to restoring peace, calm, and breath to those moments in life that take our breath away.

4

BEYOND BEHAVIOR

If you can help a child, you don't have
to spend years repairing an adult.
JOYCE MEYER

She's such an amazing, toxic, soft, guarded, defensive young lady. She's a cocktail of emotion and experience. Her story is not what fairy tales are made of. My heart breaks for her. Even in her defiance toward authority, my heart bleeds compassion.

She sits across from me at my desk with a soft scowl, a defensive front that shouts, "I am as tough as nails." When the first empathy-laced arrow from my spirit takes flight, it connects and penetrates her armor. She's in tears now. She's fragile. She's broken. She's looking to grasp onto something she can call her own with a promise of never fleeing.

In her life, nothing stays—not friends, not family, not joy, not happiness. It's why she keeps her expectations locked in her luggage, right next to the keepsakes from her mom, tucked under clothes gifted to her by seasonal adults who cared that day. She's learned that if you never unpack, it will save you the time of packing it all up again.

She treats her emotions in the same way. She's learned that if you never get your hopes up, the disappointment of being let down doesn't hurt as bad. The emotional drop isn't as steep. So, she stays guarded. She will never let you in, and nothing comes out of the suitcase, either. Her clothes will never hang in a closet, you will never handle her hopes, her traumas will never be made visible to anyone. Everything stays protected. It's just easier that way. It's part of the "how to protect yourself in the foster care system" survival kit.

I read her like an open book. I read her like I wrote the book myself—maybe because, in some ways, I did. Although parts of her demeanor and experiences are unique to her, we share commonalities and traits that suppress healthy emotions, especially wearing masks. We call this "coping."

Do you recognize this child? If you were to close your eyes, what student, mentee, or athlete comes to mind? The U.S foster care system has oversight of roughly 700,000 children. As staggering as those numbers are, I think it would be more shocking to identify the number of educators who have misdiagnosed "problem child" for "hurting child," the number of coaches who have assumed "no home training" instead of simply "no home." It's tough to quantify the exact number of unqualified educators, even though every school district or agency surely schedules the appropriate amount of in-service time in order to check the box. I'm not being cynical here; it's an honest, intentional effort to meet the social and emotional needs of all students.

The call to action and implementation of what you learned in the in-service, however, never comes in an air-conditioned room while you read a "save the world" pamphlet. Chances are, the best opportunities to implement what you learned come in the middle of a lesson or at practice, and "that child" is being a nuisance. This plea for help disguised as misbehavior hits a trigger in you, the educator, that results in lashing out or sending the student away.

Thus, the cycle continues–perpetually. The rejection, the emotions, the guarded soul, the hidden baggage shoved in a suitcase—it all persists.

RENTAL STUDENTS

Foster care can be a lot like the rental car business. Instead of cars, though, it's powerless children with mature spirits. They have indeed processed the business model. They get it: "I am a rental, and as soon as the driver's anticipated journey ends, I get returned."

Either that, or the car malfunctions–in which case the journey gets cut short and the car gets returned immediately. While that seems like a logical business model for cars, it is not so for children. Although not all 700,000 foster kids have this experience, many do. Clearly, that was the case for Sarah.

"I'm fine," she says. "I didn't need that class, anyway." She looks through me when she speaks, as if I can be replaced with anyone. As though I'm just the audience for her performance. Her words ring out like a drumline cadence: Quick, rehearsed, sharp, even bold. Everything but believable, at least to me.

Her provocative outfit gives away her false sense of confidence. How unfortunate that she craves positive attention so badly that she has fallen to peer pressure and so objectifies her body. While outwardly she might like the attention, she knows her appearance does not truly reflect her divine beauty, so she constantly pulls her dress down or her halter top up. At least, she always does around me. I take it as a sign that she respects me and that she also knows the true beauty I see inside her.

Sarah is a natural leader. It's her gift. By leader, I don't mean the ostensible leadership that's appointed, where someone bears a title. I mean she has genuine power to influence her peers. They watch her, they listen. She sets the tone of the room. In fact, that's why she sits across from me now, because that type of power in the wrong hands is dangerous.

So, I speak to her. I sit across from her at my desk, but it seems as though she feels my heart in her hands, judging by how her tears flow to the cadence of my own experiences.

I was seven years old when I left the only living environment I had ever known. It didn't matter how abnormal my primary living situation was to society, it was my normal, it was my preference. I remember telling the judge that very thing. Any alternative to my normal would have felt foreign to me.

I'm well aware that my words won't bring solutions or answers to Sarah's many questions, but at least I want to provide her with signs of hope. I know that, because when I found myself in similar peril, the answers I sought left me chasing hope, drip after drip, as if a broken faucet discharged random droplets of possibility, leaving me hydrated enough to maintain a heartbeat but with a soul still aching for more. The sense of possibilities felt faint, like a weak pulse. I had a yearning, a gravitational pull in my soul, that longed for life to return to normal.

NORMAL FEELS SAFER

My normal, as identified by my father, was extended family living. To the media and society, my normal fit the description of a "cult." I saw the definition as insignificant; I just called it home. The idea that a large group of people could co-exist under the same roof trying to combat life's obstacles seemed logical enough, especially during those most impoverished times of the 1980s. My father had well-intended goals of being able to provide resources, spiritual counsel, and overall wellness. It was a noble attempt. But somewhere along the way, the ideals behind these values got lost, which left my sister gasping one last breath and a group of young children reeling from instant displacement at an age from which it is apparently impossible to fully recover. I'm not sure any of us is fully healed. We've just moved on.

On a cold night in 1988, all forty-plus of us were removed from our group's Clackamas premises and officially started on our tour of the foster care system. Our group was too large to place everyone all at once, so the state decided to put all the boys in the MacLaren Youth Correctional Facility in Woodburn, and the girls in the Hillcrest Youth Correctional Facility in Salem. Soon after, all of us got assigned to homes in various communities.

I was fortunate enough to stay with my older brother, initially, while my younger brother and sister also stayed together. I had a lot of security staying with my brother. He was tough and rebellious, and although that might be considered a negative, it did provide a blanket of protection that I didn't know I would need (I found out soon enough when eventually we got split up). Over the next year or so, I would be shuffled through four different foster homes.

In one of my first foster homes, I remember having a fork shoved in my nose and having my nose scabbed over where it obstructed the airway to my lungs. I don't remember having difficulty breathing; I imagine I just used my mouth.

I remember another foster home, the first week feeling excited about some kids my age living there, or maybe having kids my age coming to visit (I don't remember which one). I remember we all walked to a park, and once there, a few kids started hitting and kicking me until they supposed that my balling up on the ground represented, in some fashion, the waving of a white flag. When it ended, one of the girls in our group also took a couple of swings, as if this had all been planned out.

It's odd what memories you store from childhood. Names, faces, and places fade like an evening sunset. Only the events and emotions linger for a lifetime. Like many other children in the foster care system, we are truly defenseless against our experiences. We are weeds rooted in the earth, facing whatever the forecast has in store for us that day. We cannot interrupt the storms we face.

So, after picking myself up off the ground at the park and dusting off a mixture of sawdust and despair, I walked back to my foster home with these kids, as if nothing had happened. I guess, in some ways, it never did. I never told. It was never discussed. The thunderous storms I felt inside remained as mute as lightning flashing over rainforests a million miles away. Foster care can be that way, I learned. You just brace yourself until the storm passes. So, I packed away that moment and trapped it in a large suitcase that I learned to keep hidden from everyone, even from myself.

BAGGAGE REVEALED

As I share with Sarah, she shares with me. She reveals baggage. How she was sexually abused and can't have kids. How forced prostitution ruined any chance of her having a normal relationship with certain family members. How generational desperation has ruined the fiber of healthy living.

"Nothing matters," she tells me.

My heart breaks.

Her daily choices are wrapped up in decisions by others over which she has no control. In her life, nothing has been modeled besides separation and dysfunction. Apathy is her impulse to life. Why allow yourself to dream, to set goals, to visualize a better life?

That was my response for many years. Even if you follow a blueprint of positivity, you do so with very little conviction, as if you are just humoring yourself and others. You stay guarded, clearly aware of the patterns of your circumstance. Any hint of fairy tale is a dream reserved for someone else.

This moment with Sarah does something sobering to me. Her spirit radiates an essence akin to my own experience. So, after I try to be completely transparent, she sees versions of me in her. I stand ready to fulfill my commission on earth by pouring life into her, simply by communicating the ways in which her perspective can fuel either pain or purpose. I tell her that her true source of possibility will always be her ability to persevere.

Without understanding empathy, without connecting and allowing Sarah to see me in her, and her in me, the hope she needed to feel would have remained abstract, distant. I became living proof to her that our emotional pain was the same—and that our hope could be, too.

As educators, we need to know one thing above all else: *The loss of hope opens the door to calamity.* Disruption, depression, apathy, procrastination, and cynicism, among other symptoms, are signs of someone who has lost hope. Our duty, then, first and above all, is to protect or restore hope in young people. If we fail to do that, then they will never realize the essence of their greater being.

BIRTHING HOPE

Can you recall a current or former student whose behavior you identified as a great concern? The way they spoke, how they dressed, attendance issues—such actions set off alarm bells. It's quite possible that a positive change of course can be tied directly to birthing hope where only doubt once lived.

According to *Webster's Dictionary,* hope means "To desire with expectation of obtainment or fulfillment." At a very fragile time in my life, I opened a letter that placed my soul on solid ground. Hope was restored for me the moment I recognized my dad wore the same number jersey that I did, and that he faced the same challenges. *I have a divine purpose,* I realized. While my new perspective did not provide exact instructions—life simply doesn't do that—it did provide me with hope that rang out like Sam Cooke's "A Change is Gonna Come."

But now came my Sam Cooke moment.

I confidently looked at Sarah and pleaded with her. I sought to convince her that, in fact, she had a life full of promise. It was not guaranteed, but it was available for the taking. I explained the difference between the two. I acknowledged her innate traits and attributes that served her well. How her kinetic energy could light up any room or team. How her compassion toward others could serve as a powerful conduit within a company. Even her awareness and gift of being able to influence her peers was a powerful leadership tool for anything she might decide to do in the future. I explained how all these characteristics were very promising. If used right, her journey could alter life for an entire generation after her.

There is something special about pouring life into a young person. Part of the process of grooming young minds is feeding them confidence and having them believe in an amazing version of themselves that they could not previously fathom. I saw a world of possibility twinkling in Sarah's eyes. She gazed back at me, looking both surprised and empowered. I then said that although these attributes were promising, there was no guarantee they would lead her toward a life of such fulfillment. With deep emotion, I declared that adopting the wrong perspective regarding her position in life would halt the passion needed to ignite the possibility or promise of her journey, thus perpetuating her family cycle of dysfunction, I wanted Sarah to understand a Promised vs. Guaranteed future.

We talked about her behavior and decision-making on campus, how that led her to my office on this day, what it said about her perspective–and possible ways to adjust, if she indeed wanted her promised future.

THE INDISPENSABLE TOOL OF HOPE

I have one specific tool in my educational toolbox that I always use with students: I make sure they know it's OK to mess up. They don't have to be perfect. I'll still love them if they make a bad choice. I let them know that making mistakes is a part of life. Since I can't choose what mistakes they make, I will not feel shocked when I learn of their shortcomings.

I recommend this method for all educators, because time and time again, I notice that the guard or continuousness that comes with feeling guilty dissipates considerably when you make it OK that your students are not perfect angels. You accomplish this through love and vulnerability. You, as the adult, also must be vulnerable enough and transparent enough so that they see *your* flaws.

The times I have won in mentorship—and like you, I've lost often—I attribute to my students letting their guard down, knowing they will not be judged. And although they know I will not just let them off the hook (accountability will be upheld!) I still will radiate to them an unmeasured amount of love.

Sarah was no different. She acknowledged her poor decision-making, and even implied that her decisions did not reflect the person she wants to be. I let her know that although she might have been born reflecting the circumstances of her troubled family, a life lived fully would certainly reflect the decisions she made beyond the initial cards she had been dealt. Quality, happiness, purpose, and the family of her dreams *was* possible for her, but it would take discipline and perseverance to acquire them.

I wish that someone had been there to offer me similar support when I faced a comparable storm. I was too young to identify intellectually the emotional support I needed, but old enough to know I faced my situation all alone. I recall being treated as if my educators walked on eggshells, uncomfortable and unsure about what might be "appropriate" for me.

Childhood trauma seems to short-circuit empathy in others. Those of us who lived the trauma grow accustomed to feeling as though we live in these spaces alone, that no one could possibly understand. We get treated delicately, abnormally, with nervous tentativeness, which only confirms for us our lonely and helpless situation. I think this very natural reaction perpetuates the absence of empathy, making it more difficult for trauma-stricken students, as well as for the adults who serve them. This observation doesn't, however, address the emotional reactions of students that require us to facilitate the correct tone for our learning environment. They need hope, yes, but also loving correction.

REMOVE THE TUMOR

So, how *do* you facilitate the correct tone for your learning environment when dealing with the emotional reactions of traumatized students? I suppose I could have handled Sarah's case by addressing only her actions while ignoring their root cause. Improving our capabilities as moderators of transformation, however, requires us to lessen our punitive responses to childhood trauma disguising itself as inappropriate behavior.

Far too often, we educators choose to suppress "the tumor" as a quick fix. How much better would it be, instead, to surgically remove the tumor? In that way, we could make sure a "healed" child causes fewer symptoms of discomfort, both for themselves and for our learning environment.

The National Child Traumatic Stress Network suggests that one in four children faces some sort of childhood trauma. It would be safe to say that, considering those statistics, in every class and on every team, *right now* you have anywhere from five to ten students affected by childhood trauma.

Can you name those students? Can you name all of them? Half of them? Any of them? Also, what are your "go-to" responses to remain empathetic toward their needs? I encourage you to spend some intentional time in Chapter 4 of the workbook to help heighten your awareness and sharpen the tools you need to learn to see beyond behavior.

In later chapters, we'll cover more adverse situations and how to handle them. These methods and approaches have been designed to give greater respite to you, the educator, but more importantly, to give hope to the children you serve.

FINDING A FOREVER HOME

Sarah did not find hope easily. She struggled to rid herself of the stigma that had attached itself to her because of her previous rebellious behavior and surly disposition. She abruptly left Linfield Christian Private School and finished at a public school across town. Although I wish she had finished where she started, I understand that sometimes a fresh start in life is exactly what is needed.

A new peer group and support staff seemed to fit quite well Sarah's new, evolving perspective about adversity. I don't hear from her often, but when I do, it's always about goals and objectives she has planned next for her life. She's a soon-to-be-college graduate, she's been in a stable relationship for most of college, and the two of them are planning their future life together.

Fittingly, Sarah says she wants to go into real estate, because she wants to help families find their forever home. Imagine that! I can't help but find the irony in that statement. A foster child, who has spent a lifetime living in more houses than she can count, has the desire to help others find one house with one family that they can call home, forever.

For Sarah and her future clients, I hope they find just that.

5

I TRUST ONLY YOU

Every child deserves a champion—an adult who will
never give up on them, who understands the power of connection
and insists that they become the best they can possibly be.

RITA F. PIERSON

Where is this kid?

"Our meeting starts at 9 a.m. and I haven't seen you," I texted him.

"Well, we don't have a ride, so I guess we're not coming," he replied.

I ignored the negative energy of his surface reaction and pressed forward. "No problem. Send me the address and I'll be there in 15 minutes."

Patrick begrudgingly sent the address, secretly hoping I would give up, that I would allow him to settle for behaving like the bad examples set before him. That I would just let him sleep in at his friend's house where he had been staying because things weren't going well at home.

Even though Patrick despised the parental influence that had brought him this far, his willpower and resiliency wavered at the constant onslaught of his current reality. On the outside, he looks like a student able to meet the standards and expectations set forth by educational norms. But I know different. I *feel* different. So, I won't let go. I don't so easily accept the waving of the white flag.

I remember years ago when I was in his shoes, wearing apathy like my favorite ball cap. I made sure to take it off the hook daily and wear it like a crown before I exited my home. That way, whatever the world hit me with, I would be prepared to not be heartbroken. I would expect adversity.

Armed with my own experiences from when I tried to weave through life using the tool of apathy, I ignored Patrick's defiance. I disregarded the fact that he had just missed winter finals, that he had been truant the past three weeks, and that his behavior threatened to make him a high school dropout. None of that mattered. I adjusted and did my best to meet him where he was, with the goal of pulling him up to the academic and emotional standards befitting his age.

But knowing him the way I knew myself, I first had to reach down deep to pull him up.

THE ABILITY TO *SEE* AND *FEEL*

Suppose for a moment you are back in your classroom. Class starts in an hour. It's the first week of school, so you've yet to succumb to the maddening monotony of classroom organization. In fact, you spent the night before dreaming about the perfect use of your space.

So, at 7 a.m., you are meticulously arranging the furniture for the day. You put the assignment turn-in basket neatly on the shelf, next to your desk, sitting parallel to the stapler, hole punch, and pencil sharpener. You intentionally place your stool next to the whiteboard in front of the class. You align students' desks in symmetric rows, spaced evenly across the room. Because you have teacher OCD, you even affix tape on the floor to mark *exactly* where to place each desk. *Students will have no excuse now but to keep their desks straight!* you dream.

At the exact moment that you position your color-coordinated dry erase markers to the right of the whiteboard closest to your desk, the bell rings. You feel elated. It's perfect! Your vision. Your space. Then, all of a sudden, like a stampede of excitable energy, unruly kids stream into the room and sit down haphazardly, paying no attention to the masterpiece you just prepared for them.

And that's OK by you. The pride you have for your space is eternal. You envision your room featured on the cover of a teacher magazine, with a photo of you standing next to your immaculate desk. Since it's the first week of school, it's actually a great picture of you, as well. You are months away from the "I'm over this" ladies' hair bun or the "defeated 5 o'clock shadow beard" that typically adorns embattled male teachers the week before spring break.

Now that we have set the scene of your masterpiece, how would you respond when you notice that some of your new students find it difficult to access the necessities of the room? Johnny, who broke his arm in a basketball game, cannot effectively place his paper in the hole punch and press down at the same time, because it sits on the third shelf of the bookcase and not the second. An easy adjustment for you, so you happily adapt.

"No worries," you say as you move the stapler down a row, "come as you are, we will find a way!"

Then you notice Susy, who has arrived on crutches. She needs a place to store them by her desk, so you move your stool slightly so that she may feel more comfortable.

Finally, the last student arrives. Phillip, recently injured in a car accident, shows up in a wheelchair. The rows you had meticulously put together (with tape!) to properly identify each desk space has suddenly grown too narrow. Because you understand that the needs of the child are more important than your meticulously-organized classroom, you adjust once more. Desks made of rows become desks placed in groups of six, allowing for larger row space so Phillip may breeze his way around the room.

You have just become the heroic architect of your educational setting by effectively meeting the needs of all your students. Regardless of what standards you placed on the aesthetics of your classroom, you were quickly able to diagnose, assess, and ensure that each child felt comfortable in your learning environment so that students could achieve optimal learning. Surely it helped that you could see visually how the deficiencies of your planned learning environment hindered your students' ability to thrive!

Being able to see is a remarkably powerful ability. It allows you to keep the same goal, while altering the route you must take to reach your desired destination. Really, it's no different than any other battle or challenge. In any competition, if you recognize your opponent's susceptibility in an area, you change your approach to using an offense more in your favor, thus increasing your probability of finding the win. The best leaders never predetermine a game plan before understanding the obstacles they face. Even though they never compromise their goal of winning, they change their route.

Most faculty members can visually assess the physical needs of their students and alter their game plan to effectively meet these needs. We have a high win percentage here. It's become urgent, however, that our teachers learn to *feel* as well as *see*. We are failing our students at an alarming rate because, as educators, we fail to realize that although the students we encounter might be 100 percent physically abled, their social/emotional needs are on life support. But since we can't physically see the social/emotional hindrances slowing our students' growth and potential, those needs go undetected, unnoticed.

While many students struggle with academic performance, we do not offer the same support to our emotionally inept students as we do to our physically impaired ones. Why not? We don't because the tool we use to detect them is not designed to feel or sense their dire need for emotional support.

We must begin to understand that, just as we would physically move desks to create more space for a wheelchair-bound student, so also we must adjust for emotionally impaired students. We must clear space mentally or emotionally so that they may move around optimally in our educational environment.

ADDRESSING SKILLS DEFICITS

A theory called "skill not will" suggests another way of explaining the academic deficits of problematic children. In his book *Changeable,* psychiatrist and professor at Harvard Medical School, J. Stuart Ablon, discusses his years of clinical work. He explains how he developed his theory behind students not *choosing* to be difficult. It's a condition he coined as "skills deficit."

Consider two students, Rachel and Mike. While Rachel completes all her homework assignments, Mike completes none. In most cases, both students have the same will to do the work. In other words, Rachel feels no more excited about her homework assignments than does Mike. Rachel, however, possesses the skills necessary to get them done, while Mike does not.

Ablon's research further suggests that most students have the desire to do their assignments. The result of his research really finds its significance here. He concludes that student success or failure in the classroom often comes down to the skills they have for completing tasks, rather than their will or desire. Who wants to fail intentionally? Students don't wake up choosing to crash and burn.

If it were as simple as saying "yes" or "no" to succeeding, they would say "yes," every time—which highlights the lack of skill behind the word "yes."

Ablon acknowledges that traditional school settings take few measures to address the skills deficit these students face; rather, the schools simply punish a child for not meeting the standard, which in turn magnifies their skill deficit and may lead them to lash out. His approach to change calls for schools to focus more on the skills students lack, as well as identify their underlying weaknesses. As we did while rearranging the furniture in the hypothetical classroom, we assist their progress toward optimal performance.

Think of the students in your classroom right now, those who play on your team, or form part of your caseload. How are you managing their emotional skill deficits? Are you showing up in the areas they need you most? How would you evaluate your aptitude in this category? Would your students evaluate your abilities in the same way? If you haven't asked them, how will you know?

CREATING SPACE

I found myself in that space with Patrick, having to create space both emotionally and mentally. I knew he lacked the emotional skills that could aid him during this season. It was Christmas break and the campus lay deserted. The only sounds echoed were bells and charms hanging from doors and the janitor's old radio as it did its best to cough up holiday classics, although the dominant noise was raspiness confirming it had a broken speaker.

I had set up a meeting with my assistant principal, who arrived on campus to meet with Patrick and me. She knew of the situation, and as a result, expressed appropriate feelings and empathy toward a more promising future for Patrick. She also offered a solution that would extend further than the cookie-cutter advice typically offered to our general-education population. And then the assistant principal and I laid out an academic plan that fit Patrick's situation. We provided a blueprint for him that would allow him to cross the stage with the rest of his peers.

As I sat there, I felt so hopeful. I fully recognized the life-altering moment placed in front of Patrick. I could almost see the doors that would open or close, depending on his willingness to feel uncomfortable enough to succeed.

"How can I help?" the assistant principal asked Patrick. I will never forget his response. It echoes a comment I made, still buried inside of me, when I was his age.

"Will you please tell my teachers to not ask too many questions?" he replied. "I don't want them being nosy. Will you tell them to be understanding? I might not be on campus on some days because I really don't have a home, nor do I have transportation to get here."

Behind Patrick's defiance and disrespectful demeanor lay the crux of his emotions. He wanted to be normal. He preferred to hide from his issues because being transparent provided yet another confirmation that his life was a malformed, mutated version of the fortunate 4.0 GPA's who arrive daily, drinking Starbucks and whatever else society calls trendy. Everything reminded him that he was "the least of these." So, he gave a simple response: "No questions, just understanding."

The assistant principal assured him that she would deliver the message. She also encouraged Patrick that many teachers ask questions only because they care. Communication is key, she said; we all must find someone to communicate with and to trust.

"Well, the only person I talk to is Mr. Broussard," Patrick replied. "I don't trust anyone else."

The weight of those words felt immense on my shoulders, and still does.

What student comes to mind for you when you hear something like that? What action must be taken, or series of actions must occur, in order to build such a level of trust? I know as educators we all have created such a bond with at least one student. Surely, we are all heroes to someone. Who is that student for you? And what lengths would you go to in order to protect that type of declaration from the Patrick in your world? I know I will never take lightly the responsibility of those fearsome words. I protect such words at all costs, and I hope you will, too.

LOOKING FOR ONE CARING ADULT

According to the Center for Disease Control's Adverse Childhood Experiences (ACE) study, a child needs only one caring adult to combat the negative effects of childhood trauma. That means one adult with empathy can save a child from a lifetime of perpetual negative behaviors and hurtful emotions.

I am no different than you as an educator. We can't save every child, but we can impact some. Those words, "I trust only Mr. Broussard," established the baseline of my career, my ministry. I don't mean "ministry" in the sense of converting non-believers to something more spiritual, although I am a believer. I mean ministry as in my great commission to transform young lives from hopeless to hopeful, from despair to destiny. What convicts me to do this work, even in the face of opposition, is my own journey, mixed with the cries for salvation that I hear from many students I encounter.

I have made up my mind that I will fall before scrutiny before I fall short of supporting my students. I suggest you do the same. If you are going to wake up at 5 a.m., meet on weekends, and use holiday hours to support the young people you serve, then know that, at times, you will be looked down upon, as some have looked down on me. I regret nothing, based in part on the strength of words like those spoken by Patrick: "I don't trust anyone besides Mr. Broussard."

Anyone in any profession who attempts to ascend to the brink of full potential must sacrifice greatly and risk enduring harsh levels of scrutiny. You and I are no different. We will be severely challenged. Some colleagues have called me "weird" because students confide in me and trust me with their pain. One educator described me as "an uncle" to students, in a sarcastic and judgmental way, because he didn't understand why I remained so dedicated to my students' success. Your dedication risks the same kind of treatment—but kids need a hero, and you can be that hero for them.

As we do this job, we must remind ourselves that the gift we have and the amount of dedication we possess to do this work has not been given to everyone. If our critics better understood our passion and calling, perhaps they would fight just as hard as we do, instead of critiquing us so severely. But regardless of how we are perceived by our peers or other adults, these kids need to know that they can trust us.

I know with certainty that other students have spoken words, like those Patrick uttered, to other coaches and educators across the country, to dedicated professionals who have a strong conviction about their craft. It's the ultimate testament to who you are as an influencer of young people. It's your crowning moment, your Mt. Everest summit. Even if you are fortunate enough to influence only one child's life to the point that he or she finds wholeness because of you, it's a career worth celebrating.

WHAT MAKES IT SPECIAL?

For a few seconds, allow yourself to remember the students in your life who have communicated great gratitude for your dedication toward their growth. What was it about them that made the relationship special? At what exact hour did the relationship cross over from being transactional, where you delivered a service, to relational, where you inspired excellence? Can you pinpoint that moment?

As I sat in that office, making sure Patrick felt confident enough to finish his last four months of high school, I could not help but ponder those questions. The truth is, I doubt that building the trust needed for a child to show you who they are can be earned in one solitary moment. Small occasions of gesture and big milestones of need, accumulated and repeated over time, work together to build trust.

As I looked across the table at Patrick, I felt both honor and responsibility. I also felt healing happening, buried beneath it all, in which a young, fragile version of myself sat in Patrick's chair. A sense of soothing hope was being poured into him, too. He, too, was being heard and healed. That's the beauty of being aware of your past afflictions and offering them in service to others. As you heal them, you heal yourself. Even in situations where you give everything you have in hopes of making a difference in someone else's life, regardless of the ensuing transformation or lack thereof, it's always you who benefits the most.

In retrospect, it burdens me deeply that Patrick decided not to return to school after all. The goals he desired to reach could not overcome the obstacles he faced. I felt emotionally restless for weeks after Patrick finally decided to move away from Murrieta.

Like a doctor in triage, saving young people is full of highs and lows; but unlike the operating room, I hope that somewhere down the line, the seeds I have planted will sprout and life will be born within the young souls into whom I have poured my best energy and love.

For all those who may have tried to reach me during a season when I was not ready to receive the message, I hear it now, both loud and clear. With that kind of anticipation, I remain steadfast that Patrick and those students like him will indeed blossom one day. My soul clings to the hope that, at some point, they will turn and start heading in a better and more healthy direction.

A JOURNAL NOTE

Patrick's decision to leave school prompted me to write a note in my journal, as I've been accustomed to doing since my college days. I wrote as though Patrick were the audience, although only my paper heard these words.

Patrick:

I promise I been there I kinda raised myself
No one who looked after me
I kinda praised myself
Broke and alone
I had them days myself
Went through that phase myself
No one to ask for help
Nothing in the cupboards
Just a glass and shelf
And now You in this class
They say "pass or else"
You need this in your life
Why don't you ask for help
This math can help

Health class can help
Rewrite this rough draft
Spellcheck can help
Spanish class can help
But learning becomes foreign
When they feel how u felt
Knew how your cards were dealt
When the deck stacked
Against you
No report cards can help
Excerpt from *Diary of a Poet,* "Patrick"

Although Patrick's high school journey did not play out the way I had hoped, he is doing very well. We stay in contact and, most recently while eating lunch together, he mentioned he thinks often about the advice I gave him over the years, especially as he faces the tests of real life. Hanging on to my words, he said, brings clarity to the new questions he comes up against, such as starting a new family.

As educators, we don't always get closure, but in this case, I enjoyed that great privilege. The empathy I showed Patrick in high school extended far beyond the classroom. I cared for him first as a human being, trying to connect with the challenges he faced. I met him where he was emotionally and worked to raise him up to the emotional plane of his strongest peers. What I found so rewarding during our lunch was the conviction and clarity with which Patrick now speaks about life and hardships. He says he sets boundaries and protects his space.

Knowing that I did everything I could think of to change a generational misfortune makes the work I do worth it. We are saving lives before they reach ER, prison, the streets, or the addiction centers. As influencers of the young, we are their first line of defense, the real first responders, hoping to capture the hearts of all children and shepherd them in the direction of positive dreams, hope, and perseverance.

FROM DISASTER TO SATISFACTION

Before you read the next chapter, take a moment to process the times you have helped to save a student's life from disaster, transforming it into satisfaction. What kind of emotional space were you in that allowed that type of energy to emerge? It's in that space where your inner champion is birthed, and as Rita F. Pierson says, every child deserves a champion.

I think she means that every child needs you. Not just you, but the champion you. The one who stays after practice a little longer, the one who doesn't run into the staff break room at lunch, but who instead stays in the class and starts a poetry club with students.

Regardless of how you define your inner educator champion, that is what Mrs. Pierson meant. And that is also what the Patricks in your classroom need from you. I know that such a champion lives in all of us, because that's why we entered this type of work. On the days when we feel fatigued and just want to let go, let's recall Patrick's story so we can remember to hang on just a little longer. That, after all, is what champions do.

6

ACE IT ALEX

Students who are loved at home come to school to learn,
and students who aren't, come to school to be loved.

NICHOLAS A. FERRONI

I once had a student named Alex who unexpectedly entered a season of academic valleys. Alex and I were very close. He would visit my office daily just to say "hello." Some days, he would take a piece of candy from the candy jar sitting on my desk, following the example of several other students on campus. Other days, he would stay and small talk about whatever was trending in the minds of sixteen-year-old boys. On special days, we got to speak about purpose, respect, and the pressures facing youth in today's society. Those days were my favorite. Those are the times where seeds got planted in hopes of a rich harvest.

I believe we all have that student or player with whom, for whatever reason, we have a genuine relationship, a special bond. Your pupil clings to your advice like runners clutch their water bottles on scorching summer days. That was my relationship with Alex. So, it bothered me deeply when, as a junior, he entered a season of struggle.

I received an email from one of Alex's teachers informing me of a drop in Alex's performance. The slump did not seem to bother him, the note said. A few other teachers on the email chain reported the same thing. The conversation eventually shifted to what could have brought on such a change.

In today's educational setting, an email involving multiple people is as good as a boardroom meeting. A topic gets raised and the free-for-all of response comes swift and furious. The consensus regarding Alex's academic decline? He felt tired and had lost motivation.

I didn't realize it then, but we were all *way* off.

FALSE PRESUMPTIONS

As an educator, surely you have found yourself in a position where either you or one of your colleagues presumed something about a student's actions or behavior that turned out to be false. Can you recall that time? What was that moment like? Do you periodically look back on it now as a reminder that surface behaviors are always subject to hidden emotions and circumstances?

I remember the time I benched a player for laughing after he'd made a mistake. I believed my player had not taken the game seriously enough, and decided he needed a mild rebuke. Later on, I found out he'd felt embarrassed by his performance and his laughter expressed his humiliation, not his lack of commitment. My benching the player only exacerbated an unfortunate situation. Immediately, he felt not only embarrassed but ridiculed. After meeting with the boy's parents, I gained more insight about their child and regretted my choice of discipline.

Had I known then that humans have at least nineteen smiles, and only six express happiness, perhaps I would have used a different method to handle the situation. I hope so. I already knew that none of my athletes show up to our games, set on intentionally making a mistake.

Students care about their performance, as we learned from J. Stuart Ablon's research and his insightful "skill not will" theory. Even the blanket idea of "apathy" is rooted in some form of negative entanglement. Young people are not born with a desire to fail. No one is. With that conviction in mind, we should press on as educators and never settle for surface answers. Let's look instead for hidden weeds. Let's find the root cause, and with the gentle hands of a master gardener, identify and pluck out whatever hinders our crop from thriving.

WHEN GREATNESS SEEMS OUT OF REACH

As a child, I fantasized about being the smartest kid in class, even though I often found myself in retention classes because my performance fell so far below the standard of my peers. I wanted to be the fastest kid on the playground. I wanted to have the best shot in basketball. What kid doesn't harbor similar hopes?

If all of us want to reach certain levels of greatness, then I believe the baseline ought to be the desire to become the best version of ourselves, whether we're currently perched above or below our peers. Such a level of success ought to permeate the minds of all our students.

Unfortunately for some, the ability to attain what they most desire remains out of reach. They're like a beautiful flower trapped under hardened soil, or a rocket whose misfiring engines can't move it off the launching pad. For Alex, the key factor preventing him from reaching the greatness he longed for came in the form of abuse.

The next morning, I asked my secretary to call Alex to my office. "He hasn't arrived at school yet," she informed me.

"Before he goes to any classes today," I replied, "I would like to talk with him first."

Around 10:30 a.m., in the middle of second period, Alex came strolling into my office. He appeared a little disheveled, by his standards. Usually, his curly hair shined and his outfit perfectly complemented his shoes.

"What's good, bro," I asked, "why are you late?"

"No reason," he replied.

"Well, that's not like you," I said. "Everything straight?"

My comment set him off. "Dang, Mr. B, why are you pressing me?" he demanded. "I said I'm good!"

That was the first sign that something was very wrong. Alex and I had too strong of a relationship for him to just lie to me. By then, I'd mentored him for a few years. As a freshman, this same kid would enter my office with another student, cursing the whole time. He used foul language as if it were common vernacular for a ninth-grade boy, but not at all in a threatening way. Because cursing violates my rules, however, I kicked him out of my office every day.

"Welp," I'd say, "that's a violation. I love you, now get out. See you tomorrow." I never spoke with too serious a tone, and yet both boys knew I meant business. So, they would leave and return the next day.

One day, while I half-answered emails and half-listened to Alex and his friend talk, to my great surprise, I saw them writing. "What are you guys writing about?" I asked.

"We decided it's not smart to curse so much," Alex replied, "so we have a plan to never curse again. We are writing, over and over, 'I will not curse.'" Alex then showed me his lined paper, filled front and back with "I will not curse." Although I wanted to hug them both, like a proud parent, I didn't want to come off cheesy. So, I played it low key.

"Oh, that's cool," I said. "I am proud of you guys." Inside I was screaming, "FINALLY, a breakthrough!" This type of evolving relationship with Alex created a trusting bond between us. When something felt off, I could shoot it to him straight, and typically he would be open and honest with me.

On this day, as I glanced at the morning fog still hanging over Alex's face, I said to him, "Listen, kid, I love you."

You should know that I say this to all my students, and for two reasons. First, I know it might be the only time all day someone says these words to them. And second, I really do love every kid I come across, even the students I do not know very well. I feel a great love for who they are, in that moment, and for who they can become in the future. I am deeply in love with their transformative process; it is my life's work.

I let Alex know that his teachers and I had grown concerned about his grades and that we did not want him to fail his classes. They had noticed the sharp decline from his former marks, and it worried them.

Alex said nothing. He wore a sheepish grin while his eyes looked down and to the corner, as if he were trying to look at his right jawbone. I've often seen that look. It usually signals a pause before Alex becomes transparent.

"Well," Alex said slowly, "I haven't been getting enough sleep because things at home are tough right now."

"I knew something was off, because those shoes don't match that shirt," I replied, "and the Alex I know ain't going out like that. Unless you have a girlfriend now and you don't care how you look."

Alex laughed a guilty laugh and said, "Yeah, I was rushing this morning. I didn't care what I put on."

After a few more jokes and laughs from both of us, Alex eventually exclaimed, "Mr. B, I don't know what to do. My dad's brother recently moved in and he drinks every night. Nothing bad has happened yet, but he grabbed my little brother once because he was being too loud. My dad works, so he's not around all the time. I am very protective of my brother and I try and stay awake to make sure we are safe. My uncle is just an angry drunk, and he curses and talks to himself a lot. When I come to school, I just can't focus. I am tired. I am afraid to tell my dad, because that's his brother."

At that moment, Alex's drop in academic performance suddenly made sense. Apathy had nothing to do with it. Disinterest had nothing to do with it. Rebellion had nothing to do with it. A volatile situation at home had taken a toll on his young body and mind, and maintaining his teachers' expected academic benchmarks at school seemed the least of his worries.

A NEEDED SHIFT IN FOCUS

Benchmark exams and playoff pursuits tend to afford educators and coaches few opportunities for social/emotional breaks. How could they? We stay far too busy going after performance-driven goals.

At my worst, I am as guilty as the next person, plowing through data goals and overlooking the emotional needs of children, as if they were debris on the racetrack of expectancy and self-gratification. I notice them only in my peripheral vision. At my best, I work to disassemble this cognitive norm of student engagement, deflate the pressure gauge of high performance, and allow my students to just *be*. If I were being honest, those latter moments are equally self-serving as the former ones—but there is a difference.

My focus shifts. I substitute the artificial gratification generated by meeting rubric metrics and gaining peer adulation, for the fulfilment of my true being, my true calling. I work to heal and make whole young people, allowing them time to recalibrate their lives so that they can reach a better place. Seeking my destiny also allows me time to feed the spirit which lies buried inside.

From Day 1 in 2003 when I started in education, this has remained my core desire. It continues as the underpinning of my deepest vocational yearnings, rich with the hope of wielding true influence and sparking genuine transformation. I feel truly gratified as I furnish young people with resources to find wholeness.

Calling is why artists create, athletes compete, and educators teach. All of us were born with a desire to nurture and a gift to provide.

Can you identify that moment for you? When did your "Alex" come to you, emotionally disoriented and looking for help? Because we serve a high number of students, sometimes we just miss these opportunities. I know I do; we all do. But can you name a time when your intuition allowed you to slow down from the rush of meeting the day's objectives and lean in more intimately to see and hear the true yearning of every child for assurance, safety, shelter? As an influencer, what are those moments like for you? And more importantly, how often do you experience them? What contrasting feelings do you have when you accomplish an expectancy goal instead of resonating with and adjusting to the heartbeat of a child?

The despondency on Alex's face after hearing of his failing grades provided a telltale sign that he needed a heart adjustment. He needed reassurance, to be heard, advised, and calmed down. Mostly, he needed to be loved. Without those emotional supports, Alex would not respond positively to the counsel, pleadings, or warnings of his teachers. His focus would remain as cloudy as a thick marine layer blanketing the sun. A deep fog holding captive views of progress forward.

The worry that overcame Alex, like the fears that overcome others like him, will never dissipate on its own. Nor could such worry be ignored. We had to take intentional measures to address the hidden issues. The poem "Child Activist" from *Diary of a Poet* highlights the emergency.

A teacher ain't a teacher you're an activist.

Put down all text and manuscripts

use that approach and

dismantle them

potential growth stops

When the rambling ends

A kid is so much more than what his grammar is

Something only known by the activist

Child humanitarian practices

ADD or SUBTRACT it

You will never find the MEAN

Regardless of how you FACTOR it

The RIGHT ANGLE is not found with your PROTRACTOR kit

That's not how u master it.

The true treasure

takes a different measure

Find answers in this open letter

You have to reach them

Before you teach them

Find a hurt heal

So it's you they feel

You might have to repeat

So they know you real

No Child Left Behind

Should be redefined

Nothing common about my core

you have to read between the lines

So much passion in my words
I was a destined linguist
So much pain in my heart
I never focused in English
So much focus on the charts
I thought teachers were spineless

We educators must understand that our students don't fully appreciate the importance of the academic objectives that lie in front of them. And we must learn to ask ourselves, "What in the lives of these students might, right now, be deterring them from achieving excellence?" I resonated completely with Alex's dilemma.

THE DISTANCE BETWEEN REALITY AND DESIRES

The life that happens beyond our school walls leaves a ripple effect that impacts our students' emotional, mental, and scholastic health. Those ripples affect *your* students, too.

I recalled from my childhood years the difficult issues that created distance for me between my reality and the desires I had for myself. I *loved* school, especially high school. By that time, I had fully entrenched myself as a popular high school athlete in Fairview, Oregon. My chosen persona provided the perfect disguise.

I was athletic, social, and hung with all the cool kids. I asked enough questions in class to pass for someone who cared. I obtained all-league honors in hoops and became the biggest flirt in my graduating class. I was *that* kid, just enjoying life . . . until worry and fear caused my joyous life to come to a halt.

A few years before this, my mother woke me one morning to tell me that my father had died. This time, she woke me up to inform me that my older brother had been arrested.

No child ever welcomes such news. Due to the seriousness of his offense, I wasn't quite sure our relationship would ever return to normal. Some of the charges he faced could easily have left him behind bars for twenty years or more, perhaps up to eighty.

Weeks later, I went to my uncle's house, preparing for a high school basketball game. Here I was, a fifteen-year-old kid, writing the name of my murdered sister on my left shoe, writing the name of my deceased father on my right shoe, and now adding the name of my incarcerated brother on the toe of my brand-new black and white Uptempo Nikes. Moments later, I arrived at my game, appearing to be just as capable physically and emotionally to dominate the action as anyone on the court.

But my journey to the game had changed me inside.

Regardless of how hard I tried to ignore it or pretend I felt normal, I was anything but. Along with trying to emotionally process my brother's incarceration, the many mentions of my family's past in the town's newspaper furnished me with a great reminder of how far I'd come. No longer the neglected kid, far removed from the awkward socialization phase to reach "normal life," I had graduated from serving as an art exhibit declaring, "boy, his life must suck." I'd found a new mask.

Like so many of us can attest, however, we can never truly run from our past. Sooner or later, what we choose to ignore and cover up has a way of forcing us to address the issues. Again.

In my case, the emotional boomerang was my trauma-filled, unorthodox upbringing. Regardless of how far I tried to fling it away, this projectile kept coming back around to hit me in the gut. I suppose a therapist might say you can never rid yourself of previous experiences. You have only one choice: to confront them. You can remain fearful of them, you can refuse to do the work necessary to produce healing—or you can do the opposite, and heal.

Pretending as though the event never happened is like ignoring the uncomfortable fact that your car manufacturer left out your vehicle's AC unit. Sure, during some seasons you won't notice. You can get by without it. But then other seasons arrive when the twists and turns of life become so hot and humid that the simplest drive becomes mercilessly uncomfortable. You can choose to fix or not fix the AC, but you cannot ignore the issue.

Difficult moments from your past become too heavy. You may hope to carry on like it's a normal day, as though you're a normal kid—but you just can't.

Weeks after my brother's arrest, my heart remained leaden. I worried about both my brother and my former life, once hidden and now suddenly exposed.

So, when Alex said, "Mr. Broussard, I can't focus," I understood. I had been there. Alex and I connected as I described to him the times life had made it difficult for me to focus. He listened as I tried to transparently, and yet appropriately, build a bridge between his reality and my own.

Over the next week or so, Alex continued to stop by my office. Not once did we discuss the failing marks on his assignments. Instead, we discussed his home life. He mentioned that he had taken my advice and had spoken with his dad about his uncle's alcohol abuse. Alex told me that his uncle no longer lived in the home. We then talked about facing fears and the risks involved in every action or inaction.

Alex had become an accomplished self-processor, mainly as a result of caring for his younger brother. He had grown wise beyond his years and did much of the talking when we met. Mostly, I just listened. I cared more about him as a person than about his performance on a benchmark. Eventually, without even discussing his grades, they improved. Soon, the cloud of worry dissipated and the normal Alex, the one his teachers and I knew and enjoyed, returned.

PLOTTING A COURSE TOWARD SUCCESS

I simply can't get it out of my head that the ACE study cited earlier insists that despite all the childhood traumas and related symptoms that can affect our students, one consistent, caring adult can alter the course of a student's life. Despite the dismal statistics that may afflict the lives of our students, we can help them plot a new course toward success.

At least for a season, Alex found the strength to redirect himself from the disadvantaged path he had been traveling. He listened during our talks, thought about his options, and began to choose a different route. His life reminds me of a coloring book.

I've always felt intrigued by the introspective element inherent in coloring books. The framework in which the medium takes place has both structured and open-ended elements. While a coloring book guides you as an artist, it also leaves enough creative space for you to suggest shades of various emotions, reflected in colors of many hues. Part of the "destination" is set, but part of it remains open to color in your own truth.

As you read on, I ask that you continue to allow my journey to serve as your coloring book—think of it as a guide to make graphic *your* journey, rather than mine. I want to help lead you in thought and allow your own personal experiences to bring forth vivid colors and authentic memories, once hidden. As I continue to show you the Alexes and Dylans and Sarahs in my life, I ask you to allow their stories to serve as line art for you as you reaffirm, rediscover, and refocus the purpose behind your work to encourage, instruct, and give hope to the hearts of young people.

Please remember that the real work here is not found in this book, but in you. That's the goal. Your work is not, nor should it ever be, about mere academic progress, although cognitive development is vital to a child-centered education. The real win behind our work comes when our students find a space within themselves where they feel loved, safe, supported, and encouraged to be authentically *them*. Let us work to identify moments where those ideals are threatened—which means that to protect the whole child, we must dig deeper than mere academic performance.

7

FAR FROM HOME

The secret of change is to focus all your energy
not on the old, but on building the new.

SOCRATES

White people are weird," she says brashly. I laugh an unexpected laugh, as if I feel caught off guard by the comment. She does her best to process her new surroundings. Gathering intel. Critiquing. Comparing and contrasting the world that abandoned her with the one she must inhabit now.

I imagine this is how a student might feel when experiencing a study abroad program in some far-off land. One moment they dwell in familiarity, and the next, every cultural norm they have known becomes utterly alien, despite the best efforts of their hard-working hosts.

Sitting in a comfortable slouch and speaking vibrantly in her native slang, she continues. "Like, first of all, everyone is so *nice*. That is super suspect. What do they want, anyway?"

She speaks as if she were relaying her analytical findings to her homeland. She continues. I listen with attentive ears and a heart surfing the emotional waves of currents I once rode--waves I am sure we all have experienced.

FEELING OUT OF PLACE

As an educator, have you ever felt out of place? It doesn't have to be a home replacement like foster care. It can simply be a new team, a new job, a new church. A new neighborhood. It can be any place where the environment brings an onset of anxiety, however mild, as you take in your new surroundings.

Deyja spoke to me from that place.

Buried underneath the jokes and sly remarks sat a student who craved to connect to something familiar—a smell, a look, a style of dress, a familiar quip. Just something that reminded her of home. In this case, that was me.

Deyja had started week two at Mesa, and with so many new things to take in, she was trying hard to digest it all. Therefore, it was inevitable, I suppose, to perceive things as, well, "weird." Perhaps "different" might be a better descriptor.

From the perspective of a counselor, I allowed her to process. I didn't give her answers. She wasn't looking for them and I refused to offer them. I processed with her. From my own experiences I asked questions that allowed her to take her own journey. A lawyer might have called my questioning "leading the witness," but I saw no harm in it. I said things like, "You mean to tell me you are from Los Angeles and you don't know any 'weird' black people?"

Deyja laughed hysterically. She then launched into a full report about her experiences back home, as if reliving each moment. With colorful detail, she described her neighbor and how she never wanted to go over to "that house" because it smelled funny with incense. Her mom would send her and her siblings to the home to grab certain items; they would always argue about who had to go.

She told me about the homeless man at the corner store who always wore nice shoes. On she went, both reliving her definition of "weird" from her past and connecting those emotions to her present. She managed to effectively bring the two worlds together. While geographically and socially they remained miles apart, the similar feelings and emotions they stirred helped to unify her contrasting worlds.

I understood that I could not solve her internal qualms, any more than I could have solved mine during my own time of adolescent displacement (which feels like a lifetime ago). She would continue to feel out of place, and everyone else would continue to appear "weird," until they no longer were. These thoughts would race through her mind until her new situation became her accepted normal.

It didn't matter that her new school and new peers provided resources and opportunities that her former community lacked. It didn't matter that the air and the pace of life in this suburban neighborhood was both cleaner and safer than the smog hovering over the bustling, overcrowded city she had escaped. Normal is comfortable. Even in dysfunction, these types of adjustments take time.

I know this because at times I, too, saw the world as weird; and in some ways, that world looked back at me in a similar fashion. I allowed my experiences to become an anchor of support as I sympathized with Deyja and showed empathy toward her remarks. As I sat before her, my mind raced through my own transitions from normal to weird, inner city to suburbs, familiar to foreign.

ANOTHER NEW NORMAL

After foster care, my siblings and my mother settled in a large, blue house that we shared with my uncle, my dad's brother, his wife and my cousin. For a ten-year-old boy, that home became my world.

We never ventured too far from it. For better or worse, the world as I knew it extended two blocks to the north, bounded by a corner market, and one block south, ending at the neighborhood park. East or west served no purpose for me during those years. My world was simply the store, the park, and my home, sitting in the middle.

At that age, you do not need much to occupy yourself—not that we had the financial means to do so, anyway. The old house required much repair. It creaked and cracked, but if you lived there long enough, you knew what to do in a jam.

My neighborhood seemed much the same. Sure, it had spots to avoid, but with experience, you knew how to stay safe when things got sticky. All of this was just normal. It was home.

I learned well some of the educational practices of the Cold War's "duck and cover" drills. Instead of hiding under desks for fear of a Soviet nuclear attack, we hid under dining room tables when danger approached. Emotional fear never gripped me, any more than it did those students who prepared nonchalantly for atomic devastation in the 1950s. This was routine. This was just life in the 1990s for families living in Northeast Portland.

I was far too young to adopt or perpetuate the social epidemic ravaging my surroundings, but my older brother seemed the perfect candidate: a young black male entering his teen years without a father to guide him, with enough of a rebellious spirit to start a cold war all on his own. Ingratiating himself to friends, forming bonds and loyalty disguised as a Blood gang member, and zeroing in on a foe that resembled anything other than his family and crew, he was by definition what so many young black males were at that time: America's worst nightmare. By the time I reached sixth grade, my mother had seen enough. Abruptly, she decided we'd leave my "normal" of inner-city life, and uprooted the family to the suburbs of Gresham, Oregon—or in the eyes of an eleven-year-old, outer space. My new world was, well, "weird."

I have no clear recollection, chronologically, of those days and weeks, and yet certain events and emotions still linger. I remember the beginning of my seventh-grade year, standing outside during lunch. It felt as if my worlds instantly went from Cortez shoes to Doc Marten boots. White and black tees got traded in for flannel shirts and Quiksilver graphics.

My first alien encounter took place on the blacktop as I stood with a group of boys during lunchtime. With the universal language of basketball, I figured I would feel right at home between those familiar lines. To a degree, I had it right; but my appearance couldn't escape my reality, or theirs. I was *different.*

"I have *her,*" one boy, chosen to be captain, exclaimed. I looked around; I hadn't seen a girl standing among us. But a moment later, it was confirmed. *I* was the girl he mentioned.

"That's not a girl, he's a boy," another boy blurted out. Not the most ideal introduction for any seventh grader entering a new school! A few laughs ensued, but mostly, my own thoughts sounded the loudest, as embarrassment rained down on me. *I am never wearing these shorts again,* I thought.

As I stood among these boys, wearing a baggy Michigan Wolverines short set paying homage to the infamous Fab 5 basketball team, I thought, *Surely, this can't be mistaken for a dress, can it?* My hair was in cornrows, an African American hairstyle that proved to be a unicorn to this diversity-challenged community. I don't recall clearly how the rest of lunch that day went. But at thirty-eight years of age, I still remember with clarity what was said, what I was wearing, how I felt, and how far away from home I truly was. Understanding the anxiety of my surroundings, it's almost foolish to think that after that moment, I could return to class and listen intently about some academic concept from a teacher clueless about the stress signals going off in my body. I don't recall with any vivid imagery, but I am sure I tried to do just that.

The same way Deyja sat in front of me decades later.

DO YOU RECOGNIZE THAT STUDENT?

No doubt, Deyja made connections like the ones I just described, based on her own plight—the same way your students sit in front of you today. Are you aware of the students I describe? Do you have them now, or did you? How did you handle their new, "weird" environment?

A study done by the Center for Mental Health in Schools at the University of California, Los Angeles (UCLA) found that empathy plays a crucial role in acclimating new students. There is no more fragile a time in a child's educational journey than the first few weeks in a new setting. Educators who intentionally welcome new families not only encourage inclusion, but teach empathy as well. We have several ways to use the vehicle of student inclusion to plant seeds of empathy, but a few key concepts cover the purpose behind any chosen action.

The easiest thing to remember and employ is something we've heard our mothers say a million times: "Treat others how you would want to be treated," otherwise known as the Golden Rule. Isn't that the heart of empathy? Putting yourself in someone's else's shoes, then supporting their emotional and physiological needs as if they were your own.

So, what would you need? If I were to ask you to stop reading and think about being a new student or new employee, how do you think you would feel in that new environment? A little "weird," right? Second, if I were to ask you to write down five ways you would want to be welcomed by your new community, what would appear on your list? I challenge you to do exactly that, right now. Take a minute to do this exercise.

I believe you will find something that educators all over the country discover at the beginning of the year while establishing rules for classroom management. The great teachers don't simply stand at the white board and read off pre-prepared rules to the class and expect compliance. As teachers, we know that students find it more difficult to follow expectations they don't own (meaning, they did not create them). So, instead of dictating a list of rules, this clever ploy allows students to create and take ownership over the expectations they will follow for the rest of the year. Of course, as the educator, you have a list of rules you need to set in place; and yet, in my seventeen years of working in education, never has a single class not come up with my exact list, with 99% accuracy. The obvious goal here is to establish guidelines and create student buy-in.

But something powerful lies beneath the surface. The secret to this approach is empathy. Students come up with answers that fit the Golden Rule model. How do I want to be treated while talking? How loud do I want the class to be while I am working? Students employ empathy to establish their needs for success in the classroom, essentially making it a universal rule for how everyone should be treated.

FIVE TIPS FOR SUCCESS

UCLA's Center for Mental Health in Schools came up with essentially the same secret. I trust that their research and your brainstorming will provide similar guidance to help you welcome new students to your campus. While the specific action steps you choose might differ, the heart will remain the same. I hope the tips below help you.

Tip 1. *Have a plan to give an intentional, warm welcome.*
Whether your work has you in the classroom, front office, or parking lot committee, have a visible plan that eases the anxiety of new students and families by giving them friendly faces to see and a place where they can get their questions answered. Don't force new families to search the entirety of your campus to get proper answers, or to be greeted warmly.

Tip 2. *Have a pride pack ready for everyone- students, athletes, and employees.*
Give returning or new student athletes a "Pride Pack" that allows them to be in uniform and feel like a part of the team. Include in this Pride Pack team-issued practice gear or uniform, small equipment like a mouthpiece, and flyers about important dates or fundraisers. You want to equip new athletes with everything they need to know to get started and feel like they belong. What's worse than being the new player and seeing the whole team in matching tanks, while you stand there wearing a shirt from your old school (or in my case, a Michigan Wolverines short set, which I discovered can moonlight, apparently, as a cocktail dress)? If you are a new employee or teacher, you might not need a uniform in your pride pack. You might consider forming a committee of colleagues and students to create your pride pack, designed to help students or employees feel welcomed.

Tip 3. *Create a team of ambassadors.*
I taught for two years in Kotlik, Alaska, in a small Yupik village.

With no stores, roads, or other infrastructure commonly found in bigger cities, the way of life there sharply contrasted from my normal. Would Deyja make similar claims as she acclimated to the suburban city of Murrieta? No doubt. The Center for Mental Health in Schools at UCLA suggests the very thing I found so useful during my acclimation period in what many call "Bush, Alaska." Ambassador teams are huge.

These teams can consist of students, parents, and employees alike, because each can offer a different perspective about the new culture and how to find one's groove there. In Alaska, I asked fellow teachers about making frozen-food purchases from a Costco in Anchorage. It turned out that they fly your order to an airstrip—or at least, the village's idea of an airport—and the pilot leaves your frozen food on the tarmac. Good to know for a new teacher who hadn't yet experienced outside temperatures colder than a standard freezer!

"Welcome to Alaska, my friend," my Ambassador told me, "keep that jacket you brought from Oregon; it will fit well under the jacket you will have to buy from here if you are keen on surviving our winters." *Funny guy*, I thought, along with confirming my inner trepidation that a black kid from the inner city did not belong anywhere near an Alaska winter. No matter how you slice it, that's just weird.

Tip 4. *Create some squad goals.*
The book *Born to Love* spotlights what social science research has confirmed: that human beings are herd animals. I suppose we all can agree that life and sanity are best lived out through a bond with an inner circle, our squad. Said another way, it helps to "find your tribe."

I am sure it's no shocker to learn that UCLA's research discusses the need for peer groups or buddy systems, which differ from Ambassadors. Creating squad goals requires you to be intentional about pairing new students with those you believe may share similar interests, and then allowing those relationships to provide social support. You might place their desks next to each other, or encourage interaction during breaks or lunchtime. The squad goal idea means giving every student on campus a squad to help them fight against the emptiness of walking alone around a boisterous campus. Since the beginning of time, who has ever hoped to walk alone? We always prefer to walk with a tribe, a group, a squad. Make it a goal that new students feel support right away with peers who can walk with them.

In that regard, club rush days are huge. A sports team, a fine arts group, a recycling club— the nature of the group doesn't matter; they all fit the squad goal concept. Within the first week or so of school, make it a priority to invite students to join a campus group, with the goal of finding support from peers who share similar hobbies, passions, and interests.

Tip 5. *Break the ice.*
I remember standing on sheets of ice as the group of Yupik Indians with whom I was caravanning surrounded me. I remember asking the elders endless questions about this trek. How did they know it so well? How often would they take it during winter? My questions served two purposes: (1) I truly wanted to gain knowledge about their way of life; and (2) I wanted to gain their trust by showing interest and value in who they were as people. I remember asking a question about the Iceberg in the distance and if it meant water was nearby. The elders all laughed. "Yes," they said, "we're standing

on the Bering Sea right now. It's frozen over." I am not sure what anxieties you have that would cause your stomach to feel like it dropped entirely out of your body, but at that moment, I realized that standing on sea ice didn't increase my trust in "bush" Alaska.

As the varsity basketball coach, I traveled with my players, in twenty-degree weather, to play in a tournament in another village some five hours away via snowmobile. Because this part of Alaska has no roads and the frozen bodies of water prevent boat rides, snowmobiles are an essential part of winter transportation. This trip, and many like it, gave me a great opportunity to "break the ice" with my players and, more importantly, with their families, who can be very private and unsure about outsiders. While I do not suggest you place your new students in situations that force them to question if they will ever see another day, I do endorse one of the final tips offered by The Center For Mental Health in Schools at UCLA, which is basically "Break the Ice."

Develop some intentional plan to introduce new students to others in their new environment, using a format that allows them to share things about themselves and where they came from. It's also great for the class to discuss the culture on the campus or in the new company. The ability to openly discuss and draw parallels and similarities during this process will highlight differences, but will also, to some degree, desensitize any ideas of "weird." I would also use this time to discuss other cultures or environments, emphasizing diversity in many forms in order to normalize and celebrate the uniqueness of humanity and our collective experiences. My two years in Alaska taught me a lot about breaking the ice, whether literally or figuratively.

WHO NEEDS HELP IN BREAKING THE ICE?

As Deyja sat in my office, I believe she was searching hard for a figurative break in the ice. We all have had that "Deyja" in our classes, maybe even two or three every year.

As an educator, coach, or mentor, who is that student for you? These students sit before you, as surely as "that document" sits before you on your desk among the clutter of Friday's frenzy and end-of-semester reports. You turn and flip the clutter, looking for "that document," knowing that it lies hidden under some huge and growing pile created by a disheveled educator. While you search for that document, quiet students like Deyja continue to hide, even as they scream emotionally to feel normal and welcomed. So often we simply don't have eyes to identify that student.

Do you recognize yours? Their social, emotional, and academic success depends on your ability to see them.

My whole first semester in Gresham, I struggled to adjust to my new climate. In my great desire to avoid becoming a social recluse, I felt enormous pressure to be someone I wasn't. My language and behavior changed, intentionally. I wore my new sentences and actions like the uniforms my former students wore at Linfield Christian Private School. At times, though, I forgot to take them off.

I recall coming home one day, walking in the door and saying, "Moooom." I stretched out my "o" sound, pronouncing it with a high nasal sound. I didn't know my aunt stood in the kitchen. She turned and asked, "Why do you sound so white?"

I felt embarrassed . . . again. My two worlds had clashed once more, and my limited experience proved insufficient to acquire what I longed for most: to feel normal, to be seen as equal.

If you have taught middle school students, then you know they just want to fit in. I did, too. Eventually, I succeeded. I learned all the tools necessary to become a cultural chameleon. Over time, I learned how to hide my authentic self in the shadows of my peers, as if I were a complementary echo confirming the status quo–*their* status quo.

Things settled a bit during the second semester. Although I did not recognize it then, these alternative social climates gifted me a great blessing (although in retrospect, a blessing in disguise). I learned how to appreciate and find value in all cultures. I've spent so much time within my original culture and with others that I have gathered a melting pot of experiences that have worked together to form my deep love for diversity. Eventually I found my authentic voice, my unique presence—a cocktail of diverse slang, social cues, dress, and behaviors. That is what I shared with Deyja.

WEIRD IS EVERYWHERE

I told Deyja that the term "weird" is not reserved for just one culture, but is as diverse as humanity itself. Beauty and love, intelligence and ignorance, I told her, are equally apt descriptors of individuals representing every race. I let her know the greatest gift I ever received was the opportunity to learn from so many cultures and individuals. It's the most powerful tool I possess today to help me meet the challenges of relating to the audiences I most care about: my students, and the adults who serve them.

In some ways, I had tucked away some of the stories and emotions from my time in seventh grade. I had forgotten all about the fears I'd had hanging out with people from various races. So it warmed my heart to see Deyja more at ease after our talk. As she left my office, Deyja thanked me and asked if she could come by every day at lunch.

"Of course," I told her, as several students already had a habit of doing so. She took me up on that invitation for a few days, but within a week, she stopped by less and less. On our campus of 2,500 students, I would watch her go from one social club to another. *She's finding herself,* I thought. That is the goal after all, isn't it?

Being in a new place physically produces feelings of displacement emotionally. The first few weeks, you just feel lost. As educators and moderators of social emotional well-being, our challenge lies in helping our students navigate that experience of feeling lost. We must use the golden rule and transform feelings of being alone and lost into something more productive. Use the tips above as vehicles to include new students and show them empathy whenever they enter our "weird" world. In many cases, as in Deyja's, intentionally breaking the ice can quickly turn "weird" into "wow." Developing your students' appreciation for a more expansive, broader understanding of culture and campus creates a more fulfilling experience for all involved.

8

COPS ARE BAD SOMETIMES OR NEVER

There is power in understanding the journey
of others to help create your own.

KOBE BRYANT

"I'm not racist," she said, tearfully. I listened and felt so conflicted. Her words abetted division while her heart ached for cohesion. Surely, the coronavirus was not the greatest threat to our country during the spring and summer of 2020.

While the leaders of our nation spoke with certainty about their plans for finding a vaccine, in the interim they introduced safety measures. At the same time, the complexities of race relations remained a conundrum across our nation. From the White House to my house, unified answers for equality remained segregated at best, and non-existent at worse.

I watched an uneasy reality being born inside my students for the first time in their lives. Experiences and opinions in the homes of my African American students contrasted sharply with those in other homes, particularly with their white classmates (although that statement is no more absolute than the title of this chapter).

Unfortunately, Linda's education had not prepared her for this world, this climate, this season in our country. Neither her algebra class nor her teacher's office hours had equipped her to function effectively in a season when internet memes define and protect equality. She belongs to a generation where social service is being fought using social media, and picket signs have become posts that duplicate themselves every time someone hits the share button. The sad part? So much of social media gets used as clickbait. The author wants an emotional response; the engagement itself is the win. Thus, a lot of what we see on social media belongs in the funny papers, a reality young people like Linda are still trying to understand. So today she is in my office after discovering racial equality is no laughing matter. The exact opposite, actually, as she wipes away both tears of sadness and droplets of anxiety.

My athlete's cry typifies young people across our nation. Not only are they being forced to process racial injustice for the first time, but they must do so using a platform unlike any generation before them. This reality feels both liberating and dangerous.

In decades past, our nation could debate the meaning of "all men are created equal" by private dinners inside the home, or loud marches outside of it. But becoming educated about the power of voice, and how to lend that voice in trying times, has never happened online while scrolling between selfies and envious "my life is better than yours" celebrity posts. As a result, our young people find themselves defending a cause that appears more contradictory every time they hit the refresh button on their device.

That excruciating plot highlights the phone call I made to my athlete, Linda.

"Mr. Broussard," she protested, "they were saying all cops were bad, and I was saying on my post, 'that is not true, maybe some of the things that happened to the victims were their own fault.'"

Hundreds of angry replies later, her post brought deep anxiety to Linda's heart. The hate, the constant barrage of "you are a racist" responses, left her feeling defeated.

FEARING TO TALK TURKEY

On the other side of this divide lies a workforce of educators who fear to talk turkey to a generation starving for insight. In a room full of administrators, we discussed this very climate and how we might shift the norm. How could we bridge the gap? Afraid of saying the wrong thing and overcome with emotion or feeling uncomfortable, many of us said nothing. These realities eclipsed the idea of neutralizing the anxieties and stresses our students face during this season of social unrest.

As I sat and listened to educators discuss their fear and their lack of principled action, my insides felt uneasy. As I began to speak, I realized my outsides looked uneasy as well. My voice shook because of nerves, but I felt determined to speak for Linda. I spoke against the notion that feeling uncomfortable supplied a reason not to use one's voice. I advocated for speaking up on tough topics, regardless of whether you feel it's "your place." I spoke about being vulnerable and facing fear. I wanted the room to understand that taking a stand and being a hero for kids will never feel comfortable. I let them know that we take a bold stance for advocacy and equality, not because we don't fear the risks, but because we feel the risks, we know we will be judged, and yet we choose to speak love anyway.

That's bravery. That's boldness. It does not come in the absence of vulnerability, but in the presence of it. That is what we are being called to. That is why we stand up against all wrongs. In the history of humankind, no act has ever been called "brave" or "heroic" that has lacked a sense of vulnerability or fear. Dr. King, Mandela, Lincoln, and the unconquerable little Ruby Nell Bridges, were all heroes who stared vulnerability and fear in the face. But instead of succumbing to it, they allowed it to liberate them.

HARD ADVICE

How often do you intentionally put yourself in the emotional state of fear? My guess is not often, and surely not intentionally. It's not human nature to do so. However, to become better equipped and conditioned to have uncomfortable conversations and have a willingness to speak louder than the fear you feel inside, you must put yourself in that position. That is how I advised the district's leadership team, and that's my advice to you.

To groom stronger, bolder leaders, we educators must find ways to make common practice the idea of feeling vulnerable and uncomfortable. Let's create exercises and scenarios where educators must face the challenge of making decisions amidst the turmoil of emotional adversity. Let's make "uncomfortable" more common.

We hear countless stories from life coaches and self-help gurus about the benefits of living in the space of our fear. We contemplate the idea of putting ourselves in foreign environments and how that helps us grow emotionally and increases our ability to be bold.

Will Smith has a telling video on YouTube in which he discusses fear versus danger. He calls fear merely an emotion; it exists in our minds alone, whereas danger is a real thing. So, we must evaluate dangerous situations, but we do not have to live in fear of them. Fear is a choice, he says. He ends his video by jumping out of a plane, a parachute on his back. The whole message speaks to my spirit (right up to the point where he jumps out of the plane).

I applaud Will's journey, but certain things just don't fly with me. Arctic Ice baths, running with the bulls, walking across hot coals— all these activities have been used to help people consciously face a fear, embrace the emotion, and find a place of comfort within it.

A year ago, I started taking salsa dance lessons. The emotions I faced felt identical to the ones described by educators within the room as they explained why they feared to speak on the racial issues to "the Lindas" of our school community. On Day One of my salsa journey, I remember feeling overcome with these new, foreign concepts. *Why does everyone in this salsa class make this look so easy,* I wondered. Then came the anxiety. I haven't felt that level of discomfort in *years*. I had zero experience with the music, language, culture, or moves being taught.

And I loved it.

I think I loved it from a competitive standpoint, because I was by far the worst dancer in the class. As a former athlete, nothing gets me more determined and locked in like a healthy challenge. When the class ended, everyone tended to stick around for social dancing and improving their skills. I did not dance with one person all night. I sat and watched. I learned. I familiarized myself with all the nuances of this brand-new world. At some point, the instructor came over and asked about my first day.

"It was God-awful," I replied. "I know how to dance, but this isn't dancing; this is like a tribal call, a secret handshake among a closed society."

Once she stopped laughing, she said "I am sorry, I guess it's not for everyone."

When I replied, "Well, see you next week," she gave me a surprised look, as if she were expecting anything but *that*.

The truth is, salsa was fun enough and challenging enough for me to remain in that place of vulnerability. I wanted to learn how to communicate within that space of Latin dance. Why should that be any different than educators communicating through the space of social injustice?

Yes, It's uncomfortable. It will make you vulnerable. Some educators may have zero experience enduring or advocating for the real issues of injustice because they have never had to. Because of our value system and vocational choice, however, it should hit us all like salsa class hit me—like a challenge, like an inspired decree recognizing that the other side of this level of fear brings freedom for ourselves, along with our students.

In some ways, this is the most challenging part of empathy. It forces us to embrace a fear of something unknown. Given the context of racial inequity, it will challenge what we know. That is what Linda is being forced to do. It is what our whole country is being forced to do, educators included. We are all being forced to recognize a reality we would prefer did not exist, like the email that just came through ten minutes past your time to go home. We ignore this part of empathy because of what it suggests about our country, our nationalities, communities, neighborhoods, our families, our brothers, our sisters, our homes, and even ourselves. The number of individuals who intentionally self-audit their cultural sensitivity and awareness is exceedingly rare. It is imperative, however, that as influencers of young people we do just that, even at the risk of being forced to realize that the position in life where we sit provides an obstructed or unobstructed view of this thing called "The American Dream."

THE WAR WITHIN

If the first part of empathy is "to understand," the next part is "to share the feelings." The understanding part causes war within us. For me to understand you, I must first process what I see through what I know to be true. It is easier to do this when you do not have a preconceived notion of the experience.

If you had never visited Bush, Alaska, for example, it would not be that hard for you to understand my position that Alaska is a cold place; that would not create a war within you. You would take my word for it. Had you been to Alaska in August when it gets much warmer than in January, however, you might perceive my perspective as in conflict with your own, which produces an emotional unrest inside of you.

To push further through the theory of understanding and its impact on empathy, I think we can all agree we truly understand only ourselves, and it takes a great deal of time to truly even know that well. We are ever-evolving. As an African American male from Oregon, I cannot explain more accurately what it is like being a Yupik Indian male from Alaska than can a Yupik Indian male. A country-raised Hispanic female from Idaho cannot tell a Hispanic female who lives by the border in South San Diego what her California experiences are like, or what pressures her family may feel. We find ourselves employing empathy, not based on the understanding we get from others, but by the understanding we want to give others based on our position in life. Although this is natural to do, we must resist this urge and embrace a reality shift as our students and colleagues speak their truth.

I recall my trepidation over asking my brother to pre-read a few chapters of this book, especially those that pertained to him. My fear came from the worry that he would not accept my truth, my position and view of life, and how I understood it all. How I understood him. What I found both surprised me and eased my fear. He responded with a welcoming and contrite spirit, full of empathy. He said he felt moved emotionally about my perspective because he did not know that I understood our journey together the way I did. Without question, the only way my brother could reach that perspective was for him to rule out any position or viewpoint that would accept my experience only if it confirmed his own. He chose to take my experience and allow it to stand on its own, and not as a competing force against his. I love him for that. He continued to view life through the lens of his hardships, but he did not force his perspective on me. He allowed me to interpret life from my own vantage point.

And that brings us back to Linda's dilemma and how it reflects the social quandary facing our country during the spring of 2020. All across the United States, people like Linda tend to doubt any perspective that fails to reflect their own personal economic, religious, social, and regional experiences. Empathy does not do that. Empathy requires us to sideline our own experiences in order to embrace the attempt to understand the experience of someone else, and then allow authentic, appropriate emotion to flow from that place.

NEW SHADES OF GRAY

So, there I was, a black male educator, softening the cries of my white female student. I embraced Linda's questions and thoughts about why cops are good, which they are. About how much good they do for our community, which they do. Also, why a blind belief that all cops are bad infuriates her, which she showed.

To support her truths, I had to widen her lens to cover more of a universal social climate. I had to explain that the slogan "to protect and serve" varies in meaning around our country and has for some time. I explained that what it means to her, in her neighborhood, could mean something completely different to someone growing up across town.

I encouraged Linda to do some research to help her understand why some respondents pushed so hard against her claims that equality is everywhere, and to consider whether it might be more fair to say something like, "equality is everywhere for a white female living in her city and neighborhood." I had the opportunity to discuss with her an article from the British Broadcasting Corporation (BBC) that stated black people in the U.S. are eight times more likely than white people to be stopped and searched by cops. This reality leads African American families to make sure they have "the talk" with their young sons about how to handle questioning by a police officer. "The talk" is given as early as age twelve and is often described as "a rite of passage." I tried to help her understand that fear, anxiety, and mistrust in race relations is commonplace in some neighborhoods across the country.

Pushing further, I explained that holding a badge has not translated to uniformity of equitable treatment for all citizens. I acknowledged her experience with heroic officers in uniform. I also enlightened her on sinister motives lurking behind that same shield, as in the case of convicted officer Derek Chauvin, found guilty in the death of George Floyd on three counts (second-degree unintentional murder, third-degree murder, and second-degree manslaughter). Officers are universally different, I said. No two officers are the same, and in some cases, vast disparities exist. I explained that the reasons behind the disparities range in nature. Some are innocent human misconceptions, while others are rooted in the soil of our country's historically unequal application of "All men are created equal."

Together, Linda and I discussed the just treatment I have received from officers while living as an African American educator in Murrieta, California. I cannot, however, speak to the experience of the financially strapped father of three living in low-income housing in the heart of southside Chicago. I told Linda that, according to the BBC study, black people are six times more likely than a white person to be killed by a law enforcement officer. I saw Linda's eyes widen as she began to see that her personal experience did not qualify as "the" experience for everyone. I tried to spoon-feed Linda in a way that she found digestible, and less of a threat to her perspective. She began to see that her perceptions can diverge, even radically, from another's experience. She began to understand that her view and vantage point may differ enormously from that of other students her age but who lived in another community, or who lived in the same community but were of another age, race, or gender.

Her very militancy about her belief system and perspective, I believe, enabled her to begin to have empathy for those whose experiences afforded them a very different perspective. In the case of current American racial tensions, many wildly dissimilar perspectives tend to take the same militant stand, battling it out on the picket lines of social media. Her new, introspective journey permitted her black-and-white worldview to admit new shades of gray, which brought us full circle back to the attack she was experiencing and why a softer, more empathetic position would have served her better.

TAKE A WIDER LENS

To address these times of racial divide, I think we must start by acknowledging that they exist. Even if they do not exist for you in your world, it may exist for someone else in their world. We must use a wider lens, like I did with Linda. We must find a space where diverse experiences breed diverse thought. As educators, that is our task.

Once we can agree and accept that we all have diverse experiences, we can then discuss the emotion behind our experiences and support each other from that place. We seek a place of empathy, not a place of competition. We must educate ourselves and others that the perceptions of others do not make our perception false. In addition, we should not feel threatened by someone's vantage point, but in fact, we should employ empathy by doing our best to truly grasp it. That is where harmony begins, when we authentically embrace someone else's understanding. Such an embrace can subconsciously challenge us to continue widening our lens.

We *must* go there. We must allow *both* to exist. We must understand that both *can* live simultaneously. Talk about it. Understand it. Empathize with it. Resolve it. And allow it to heal. A process like this takes us along a path of vulnerability that fosters growth. It's either that or ignore the topic altogether, forcing the Lindas of the world to remain restless and distressed.

What stance will you choose as you employ your podium of influence? I hope, for the sake of our future communities, that you choose to be vulnerable, to fight against fear, to embrace your inner "Mandela." Lead your young people in all the conversations they need you to lead for them to be liberated, so we can all be liberated. In the end, you will be remembered for "being" something. Make that "something" a reputation for boldness and bravery.

9

DYSFUNCTION IS DISTRACTION, DISTRACTION IS DISDAIN

Everything you do in the day from washing to eating breakfast,
having meetings, driving to work...watching television or deciding
instead to read...everything you do is your spiritual life.
It is only a matter of how consciously you do these ordinary things.
LAURENCE FREEMAN, *Aspects of Love*

As I sit in my office, my heart breaks. Two students speak loudly, passionately, just outside my door. One student is trying to encourage the other. One says she doesn't know how to handle the things she's facing. The other shares her story.

"You can do it, because I did," says one student to the other. "I spent fifteen years without my mom, in and out of jail she went. I don't even know my dad. My uncle was my father figure, and he's now spending ten years in jail."

They discuss being "closed in" and "not open." They exchange numbers and offer each other support. It's beautiful how transparent they are with each other, despite how painful their conversation is to hear. It's even more painful to realize that this is their *life*. To think that they have school tomorrow, they'll have assignments and will be asked to achieve, as though the biggest stresses they face are pop quizzes in history or assignments in social studies.

From the sound of it, both students are very mature. They have strength beyond their age. It's a great reminder that we don't know the battles others face. Also, that we had better be thankful for the lives we do have. Somebody, somewhere, faces a battle we can't even imagine. I'm praying for our youth.

What you just read was the gist of my social-media post of February 4, 2020. In some ways, the two young ladies who sat on the floor outside my office that night represent the difficult experiences of all the students mentioned throughout this book, as well as the countless students I chose not to highlight but who suffer similar plights. They also represent *your* students and your experiences.

We simply don't know what disasters have manifested in our students' lives, which, in the process, have caused major educational distraction. What we do know is that our students often fall short of our expectations and that we disdain how distracted they are.

For their sake, I caution against that.

For your sake, I caution you.

I understand how easy it is to overlook a student in distress who gets pulled over on the highway to achievement. In some fashion, it's done every day on highways across America. You notice a car with its hazard lights on, but with little thought about stopping and lending a helping hand. Yes, some hidden danger could lurk there, and so your intuition for self-protection comes into play.

A very similar scenario gets played out in classrooms every day across our nation. As an educator or coach, you have an educational objective for the day, a scholastic destination you want to reach. Your road map didn't plan for a student "pulled over" emotionally, hazard lights flashing (or covered), causing a delay. What you see is a distraction to your learning environment.

What you do next is crucial.

That classroom moment is as pivotal to preserving life as our experience on interstates. Unlike the possibility of you becoming a victim on the side of a random highway, however, the only potential victim in your classroom is your student. *That's* the danger.

Will you notice the distress signals flashing all around you? Will you care? Will you pull over? You and I, like many educators, arrive daily with a destination we want to reach. I have yet to see a lesson plan of any kind that include something like, "Be prepared to detour for oncoming distractions." Like any driver, we set our sights on a destination, and any distraction becomes a hindrance, whether consciously or subconsciously. As a result, we feel disdain for the distraction and its cause, without spending much time analyzing why our students have created a traffic jam for themselves and for others.

I wish I could say that I have avoided this poor pattern of behavior, but I can't. All of us, myself included, have been *that* driver in the classroom. At times, we are so laser-focused on the pressures of performance-driven tasks that we just miss it.

On February 4, 2020, however, I didn't miss anything. The words of the two young women echoed outside my office and pierced my heart. In the middle of scheduling games and typing reports, I froze. I listened. My spirit felt deeply moved. Stories of stress, distractions, worries that feel like literal weight placed on my shoulders, is the only way I can explain it.

I've been there. The family dysfunction, I've been there. The loss of siblings, I've been there. The incarceration of uncles who served as father figures, I've been there. The incarceration of siblings, I've been there. The disruption of personal security becoming so severe that scholarly discipline or focus feels like an impossibility, I've been there.

THE PAST BECOMES PRESENT . . . AGAIN

At some point, as I listened to the passionate conversation on the other side of my office door, my emotions accounted for the dominant noise in my head. As the girls continued to cry out to each other, a sudden onset of past personal trauma made the students' decibel levels grow faint. My past suddenly became my present.

It felt as though I were again navigating my way through my high school years, both as a popular basketball player and as a hidden soul. Almost twenty-three years ago to this moment, I received my brother's letters from jail.

I feel quite positive that I drew the ire or disdain of most, if not all, of my coaches during these years. Same for my teachers. Sure, as a respectful kid, I rarely dished out blatant disrespect. But I was very distracted. I engaged and applied myself only as an afterthought. At best, those attributes became back-seat drivers to what really drove my attention: distress.

I remember showing up to school a few days after my brother's arrest, feeling like the whole world knew that *my* brother had shot up the city in reckless pursuit to either chase or run away from his demons (I'm still not sure which). But it was worse than that. After the town and state newspaper connected Eldridge Broussard the 3rd (my brother) to Eldridge Broussard the 2nd (my father), and the infamous history therein, that knowledge also became my paranoia. Nevertheless, my instructors still asked me to remain as mentally sharp as every other Johnny and Sally attending our school.

From the outside looking in, I suppose I had no excuse but to perform in an expected or favorable fashion. I was one of the stars of the basketball team, after all. My peers liked me. I was charming enough to disguise my discomfort in any social setting, something I learned during my elementary and middle school years. Even up to the night of my brother's arrest, I was being crowned as homecoming prince in front of 2,700 of my closest peers and their families, or whoever came to the homecoming game that night.

Within hours, that would all change.

My brother sat behind the wheel of a blue Cadillac, primed for a *Godfather* sequel, racing down the busiest street in town and pulling the trigger on both his foes and on my disguise. After the ricocheting bullets landed, after the pursuing band fled, after my brother's body went limp due to the force of impact as it hit the steering wheel, after his car wrapped around a light pole like a tight hug on a still night, my comfortable life became very uncomfortable.

I didn't sleep much that night. Call it selfish, but the honest truth is that my mind raced for as many reasons concerning my own life as it did for my brother's, as he sat in some downtown jail cell. I know that's selfish; I guess you can consider it a bad omen for all high school kids. But the stress is real. The distraction is real. You simply can't focus.

As the two girls outside my office discussed their pending obligations, I reflected upon my own from that night of my brother's arrest. I remember dreading the call to my girlfriend the next morning. I had to let her know that the dance we'd spent the last month obsessing about would not happen. No way I could show up to that dance, only to undergo the scrutiny that I knew would ensue. Looking back on it now, the intense degree of fright over that possibility might have been self-imposed. But what did it matter? Stress in the moment is still stress. I simply didn't know how I would go to class, go to practice, float around campus from peer group to peer group, as if I were some carefree, jovial kid looking for reasons to laugh and make you laugh. That was the spirit I embodied. During that season as a sophomore, however, my spirit got arrested along with my brother. I just couldn't escape the onslaught of mental pressures that descended on me during that time.

The same kind of onslaught these girls face now, I thought. Still, I didn't want to move, get up, be used, or be exposed. I didn't even know who sat on the other side of that door. I did know that I had attached myself to their voices, as if they were my own. Here I was again, talking to myself: "So, you are just going to sit here and not offer support in ways that maybe only you can?"

Reluctantly, I detoured from the plans I had for myself. I minimized the computer screen of distraction and marched toward what really matters: saving lives. I opened the door and immediately recognized the two ladies: two of my athletes. I knew them, but I didn't know their stories. As an educator, that's metaphorical in a way, right? Such a literal and figurative moment for us all. Knowing our students, but not their stories. Seeing their faces now, however, and connecting the dots, their stories suddenly made sense. The fights, the emails from coaches, the distractions they had created across campus. It all made sense now.

The moment I opened the door, the more brash of the two students, who wears her heart on her sleeve, quipped with a raised eyebrow, "You were in there the whole time."

I felt bad. "Yes," I said, as I placed my body against the wall and slowly slid down to a sitting position. I wanted to arrange my posture as if I were them, at eye level. For a moment, I wanted to rid myself of any titles or perceptions of authority. I simply wanted them to know I saw their hearts. I also wanted them to see mine.

"It's going to be OK, you know," I said. "The two of you are powerful. Strong. I know this, because I am you. What you are facing now will help you overcome any adversity you will ever face. You will have an advantage in how you perceive storms in life. You will be prepared and ready for them. I tell you this because I went through the same challenges you face. What people don't know about me is I, too, was in foster care. I've had siblings and parents die. I've had loved ones go to jail."

Once I said this, I saw walls begin to break down and guards drop. At that moment, they no longer looked at me as their Athletic Director. They looked at me simply as someone who understands. What I did next, I rarely do. I read them part of a poem.

I wrote this particular poem after leaving a lunch with my older brother and sister on one of my visits back home to Oregon. I always write from real-life moments. My spirit gets overtaken in an instant and I find myself writing things down that many might submerge or share only with a confidant. I always prefer to write, even if it means sitting in the parking lot of a random restaurant, trying to capture the moment. And so, in this case. I wanted to memorialize the moment in time, realizing that we have an opportunity on such occasions to present to the world the grace, intelligence, success, and strength that can emerge from responding effectively to a hidden journey of pain and dysfunction.

> *If you knew*
> *Really knew*
> *What this 3, been through*
> *You would question, everything*
> *except Jesus, too*
> *The world, dropped the ball*
> *But Jesus, came through*
> *I mean, no dreams*
> *Just screams*
> *And sirens, that turn blue*
> *Damn our past*
> *Lost our dad*
> *Saw my sister, killed too…..*

I shared the poem, I told them, because I wanted them to know they were not alone. We spoke about navigating the distractions, handling the pressures. How sometimes, just showing up is a win. Just go to class. Go to practice. Let your attendance be enough for today.

I also told them that I hoped they looked at me as hope. That although they were born reflecting their parents' decisions, they will die reflecting their own. Their degree, their success, the stability of their future family, all will reflect the decisions *they* made. I let them know how blessed a life I live now and how I arrived here. How I overcame adversity myself. Their body language changed dramatically as I saw empowerment and possibility seep into their posture.

In that moment, for me, it was all worth it. All of my issues twenty-three years ago were worth the price of potentially saving these students. I would trade nothing. Having the ability to empathize with these young athletes in a way that sparked hope felt euphoric. It is also my calling.

The next morning, like bashful elementary school kids, these two brash high school girls tiptoed into my office.

"Mr. Broussard," they said. "We were wondering if we can have that poem you read to us yesterday. It meant so much and it made us feel better."

"I would be honored to share it with you," I said, "and I want you to know that I will always be here." They started coming by my office regularly, just to check in. Even though I have a busy office and the tone and depth of our conversations would vary, I knew why they stopped by. Their visits went unnoticed by their peers, and that's OK. I also had once walked in their shoes, trying to avoid being seen.

IDENTIFY THE MOMENTS

As educators, we should strive to identify opportunities like these. I had no plan for that moment that included sitting on the floor with two students and putting away the deadlines of my world. I had zeroed in on getting reports done. It's easy to get engulfed in such a train of thought! But I also know that while we map our course toward a certain destination, we must never toss out our ability to spot our students who face disaster, and render aid.

Yes, it can be difficult to sense those hazards, but often a student's distraction or detachment from the day's objective can be your biggest clue that a detour is required. Don't let it arouse your disdain. Reaching your desired destination is still possible; it'll just require an alternate route and take a little longer to get there.

I can assure you that, although unplanned, this route will define your career. This is our real calling. It's not *an* assignment, but *the* assignment, to meet our students in their moments of danger and to walk them back toward spaces of clear thoughts and bright futures.

TECHNICAL SKILLS VS. SOFT SKILLS

The best of who you are as an influencer of young people will always be measured by your human effect, not your intellect. What matters most is your empathy, not your intelligence. For three consecutive years, I partnered with Positive Coaching Alliance (PCA) to help with professional development, focusing especially on building the right culture on my school campus. PCA has partnered with just about every major sports group at every level in the country, including Amateur Athletic Union USA, Jr. NBA, US Soccer, USA Lacrosse, Boys and Girls Clubs of America, and the list goes on.

During those years of my partnership with PCA, I felt intrigued to learn what made a great coach. I spent an extensive amount of time with the organization's staff and mine to bring those aspects to light. During one of our workshops, we combed through data in which thousands of high school athletes wrote down on sticky notes their answers to that coaching question.

If you played a sport or participated in any club, how would you describe a great coach? Naturally, you can extend it to being a great teacher, as certainly we are coaches in our own right. What would that answer be for you?

I would describe what we found as profound, but not surprising. After looking at the responses through the lenses of technical skills and soft skills, which I'll distinguish in a moment, the answers overwhelmingly came in favor of soft skills. And yet, as coaches and educators, we can easily get distracted and frustrated when our technical skills must take a back seat to our soft skills—the very skills which drive the critical lessons home.

According to the PCA, a technical skill might be something like a coach's knowledge of the game or understanding a drill, or an instructor's ability to explain the Pythagorean theorem, demonstrating each note on a piano, or helping ESL students with English grammar. One word can define soft skills: empathy. Student athletes described soft skills with such terms as "being a motivator," "encourager," "supportive," "able to stay after practice," "optimistic," "great communicator," and "understands." In the view of students, the importance of soft skills for coaches *far* exceeded that of technical skills, by a ratio of 10:1.

The two student athletes who sat outside my office that night needed me to apply soft skills, not technical skills. My knowledge of sport, ability to schedule games and buses, my familiarity with effective training exercises and injury protocols, *none* of that was vital to their finding peace and purpose in the here and now. These students needed to be understood and encouraged. They needed someone "to stay after practice." They needed support. These students loved their sport dearly, and their athletic goals aligned well with their teammates and coach. At that moment, however, they found themselves pulled over on the highway of emotional distraction. On game day, they looked for aid. Surely, their coach did not have *that* written down when he prepared the game plan. And yet, there we were.

You can find yourself in that same place while you are in the classroom or on the court, pool deck or podium, trying to deliver knowledge. If we allow it, these moments can present us with superhero opportunities. These are the sticky note reminders that will matter ten years from now. Our students will never write down, "my coach was great because of the stellar way he designed warmups before the game." They will say, "I remember when my mom was sick, and before the game, my coach took me to the hallway, hugged me, told me he was praying for my family, and that he loved me." *That* is the story that will stick to their hearts.

Behind all the words students used to describe "soft skill" lay unheard stories just like those. Words like "understanding" point to the use of soft skills and describe the glue behind effective empathy.

As coaches, teachers, administrators—whatever your title may be in children's lives—we all show up with a game plan, a lesson plan, a to-do list. We arrive with a task in mind, and we never write down the word "distraction" as a part of our plan, any more than we mentally factor in "traffic jam" for a trip across town. For us to be most effective, however, we should do just that. Let's plan for bad traffic.

In Southern California, thousands of drivers take Highway 91 west in the morning and Highway 91 east in the evening. Without traffic, that drive would take about forty-five minutes. With traffic, however, that same drive takes two and a half hours. Most drivers who use this road do it every day, and so they leave early enough to ensure they arrive to work on time.

As experienced educators, shouldn't we also mentally and emotionally prepare ourselves to be expert "drivers" so that we can meet our educational performance standards? To be good teachers or good coaches, we must have a good understanding of our subject matter; but to be one of the great ones, we must keep our eyes on the destination while at the same time remain ready and willing to take all the necessary detours to ensure we meet the needs of every child—the whole child—without leaving anyone behind. We can do this! It just requires us to become expert drivers of our setting and destination.

As the benchmarks of life attempt to press us forward at a pace that tends to turn distraction into disdain, be intentional about keeping the pace slow enough so that you can still read the signs. Do that, and you'll allow your inner greatness to become a "sticky note" for a future champion.

10

MATTERS OF THE HEART

No significant learning can occur without a significant relationship.

JAMES COMER

I learned one fundamental truth early in my career as an educator: my students' ability to connect with the material I teach does not depend solely on my mastery of the subject matter. I have come to understand that influence and having the ability to connect is just as important as the subject itself.

The more control I have over the emotional space between us, the more my students are willing to exert themselves toward a desired result, even if I lack the ability to get them to that desired result myself. The right emotion can drive them to the desired result on their own, which, in my opinion, carries an immeasurable value. In fact, in some cases, my ability to obtain mastery over a lesson so that I can teach it effectively may have very little to do with a student attaining the goal.

I fell upon this critical understanding both sheepishly and proudly. I was fortunate enough to have an experience early on that would mold my educational philosophy for the rest of my life.

OUT OF MY ELEMENT

In 2008, I found myself applying for a pre-algebra job at Linfield Christian School, an esteemed K-12 private Christian school in the heart of suburban America (otherwise known as Temecula, California). I still remember going through the interview process, thinking, *I don't belong here. I am too young, too dark, too diverse, too poor, too unqualified, too uneducated to serve in any role here, especially as a pre-algebra teacher.*

My desperation for employment, however, far exceeded any anxieties about applying. I had lived in California for less than twelve months and all the public schools already had begun the school year. I laughed an ironic laugh upon applying, and the universe laughed back, louder, once the school offered me the job.

What have I gotten myself into, I wondered. *Surely, this is a joke.* I felt completely out of my element. How could I possibly do this job? I could not see how I could relate to either the faculty or to the students.

What transpired over the next few weeks is a lesson I hope to impress upon all educators, all coaches, anyone who sets out to serve young people well.

The school officially hired me in early August, and I began working as a pre-algebra and history teacher just days before the start of instruction. Someone handed me an algebra book that might as well have been a biomechanics manual written in Serbo-Croatian. I always struggled in math, and the thought of me teaching anyone the subject seemed nearly criminal. At least, that was my perspective, formed by my insecurities. I was determined to spend each painstaking night learning the material, with the goal of not just teaching my students, but even more so, proving to them that I was not an idiot. *No doubt, they will figure this to be a ruse,* I thought.

After the first semester of long nights and longer lecture hours, I nervously awaited the question, "Mr. Broussard, do you know what you are doing"? I remained wide-eyed as the questions never came.

And then something astonishing happened. The kids not only were learning but thriving at a very high level. In my subconscious, I suppose I concocted many reasons for this. But I benefited from one amazing reminder, as surely as I hope you as an educator will benefit from this chapter itself. The reminder is called *emotion.*

Emotion is one of the strongest forces we have to reach top human performance. For better or worse, emotion will influence behavior, whether through empathy or apathy. Emotion is a key contributor to performance. How we *feel* about someone drives how we *perform* for them.

Many over the course of history have taught repeatedly of the wise use of emotion to generate a desired response: Dr. King, Gandhi, Mandela, even Jordan, Kobe, and LeBron. While those leaders represent very different subgroups, the drive behind each of their legacies comes from the same stirring place: Emotion. Or, if you will, heart.

THE POWER OF EMOTION

Motivation is an extreme power source. We might define it as inspiration or disdain channeled and fueled toward a certain action. Every day we see how emotion generates energy and why it must be protected.

The legends of both Kobe Bryant and Michael Jordan, as told by their peers, have in common that each of them fed off the body language and energy of others. They knew how to feed their fire. At times, they found it more vital to find the right combative energy than the right juice to get the best shot. Kobe famously told about the first time he faced off as a young eighteen-year-old against

Michael Jordan, arguably the greatest basketball player of all time. The two played the same position, which meant Kobe would be guarding MJ all night. The story goes that Kobe's teammates warned him, "Whatever you do, don't look at Michael Jordan in the eyes." After hearing the statement a few times during pregame, Kobe finally replied, "Why not?"

"Because," they answered, "If you look at him in the eyes, he takes it as a challenge. He gets really determined. It's just a different level." Kobe responded to his teammates using words not suitable for this book, but I can translate it as, "I am that, too. Whoever you think he is, I am that, too. He'd better not look me in the eyes." The game concluded with Jordan's team winning and Kobe's stat line far inferior to Jordan's; but that eighteen-year-old kid's mindset never wavered. Eventually he would turn the table on Jordan as he matured into a pro.

On the surface, this story displays competitive drive at its most elite level, a burning desire to compete that rages like a wildfire. A similar wildfire rages inside the hearts of all the greats, whatever their occupation or field of competition. They just channel it toward their chosen place to conquer. We admire this quality.

But what lies under the surface? What do we find when we peel back the layers? Typically, we discover that under that uber competitiveness is emotion, a feeling that centers around the heart. Both Kobe and Michael knew that in order to be great, they had to stoke and manifest the emotion that would allow them to thrive, to perform at an elite level—even if it meant looking for reasons to get upset or feel challenged. They used peers, the press, spectators, and media clippings. They considered fair game whatever they could use as fuel to feed the emotional fire within to compete. Coaches use the same tactic to try to put a fire under their team.

I believe that we all have levels of Kobe and Michael inside of us. While some of us are more intentional than others about activating those levels, inside all of us all lie mountains and oceans of drive. I don't mean the physical drive needed to attack the basket in pursuit of Hall of Fame status. I mean the emotional drive needed to accomplish a goal. We need a why.

What is your why?

Our goal to influence young people will never change. Goals rarely change when we think purpose. Our purpose remains constant for decades. What wavers, like flickering flames on cold nights, is our emotions and motivation to keep our purpose lit. We must fight to protect that motivation.

In his book *Long Walk to Freedom,* Nelson Mandela describes a poet who came to his Methodist secondary school campus. The poet spoke words of activism that ignited within Mandela an emotional spark that he had never felt. That example of an emotional harness allowed him not only to fight the good fight, but to light an emotional spark in countless others.

If we want to retain empathy within us, allowing it to radiate through our bones and seep through to the hearts of others, then we must stay charged. Our goal is our target audience and how we want to influence them. That is our bullseye. Our emotion and drive provide the velocity needed to keep our arrows in the air, seeking the target. If we desire to influence our students to perform at high levels, then we ourselves must be dialed in emotionally. We must directly hit the hearts of our students often enough to build a relationship with them worthy of their positive response. They must feel and feed off the emotional connection we have established with them. We must allow our emotion to drive home our empathic plea.

My own colossal moment was miniscule, if you take a linear view. But without question, the incident shaped who I am as an educator. And I learned this lesson not from a colleague, but from a student.

A SURPRISING REVELATION

During a parent-teacher conference six weeks into my first semester at Linfield Christian School, I tried to enlighten one parent about her child's academic prowess. I ended up being the one enlightened.

Before me sat a colleague, Mrs. Brown, whose daughter, Allie, was a student of mine. The whole day I felt on edge, dreading the inevitable questions of my incompetence in relation to my role as an educator. Because of my past, I battled (and still battle) hurdles of insecurity regarding my competence and acumen. My two master's degrees, my undergraduate degree in K-8 Education, and my many certifications earned and tests passed, have little power over the young boy sitting in retention classes, struggling to read and do arithmetic. He still lies buried within me. It doesn't matter how far I run or what I overcame; the battle of those insecure emotions remains ever-present. I am very aware of this reality, and on that day, I was prepared to answer the insecurities of my subconscious and of Mrs. Brown, should any questions arise. But they didn't.

Instead, Mrs. Brown thanked me profusely for relating to Allie in a way that inspired her to lean into her math studies. If I were to rephrase her compliment, I might say that she thanked me for "finding the heart of my daughter, your student." I didn't know the history behind Allie and her math grades, but I did know that she worked extremely hard. Although things weren't easy for her, she never quit. Her test scores were always in the B range and she and I both felt pleased about the amount of work she invested in her studies.

"You don't understand what you have done for my daughter," Mrs. Brown insisted.

"What do you mean," I replied, a little puzzled, "she seems fine to me."

"I have never seen my daughter work so hard in math," she declared. "One night, doing homework, I asked her why she was working so hard in math this year. Allie replied, 'Because I don't want Mr. Broussard to think I am stupid.'"

That was Allie's fuel, the energy source required to drive her purpose. Like Kobe and Jordan, that was her stare in the eye. Like Mandela, that was her call to justice. She mentally found a way to manipulate her emotions to meet her goal. Allie had no goal to fail math; students never show up to class so that they can fail. It may be that they simply lack the emotional tools needed to succeed (see chapter 5 and "Addressing skills deficits").

Allie's comments, related to me by her mother, both enlightened and transformed me. I had spent six anxiety-driven weeks learning every single lesson, both inside and out, but still felt that my efforts wouldn't be enough. I had obsessed over anticipating every possible question my students might ask. I didn't want to fail them. I didn't want to fail myself. Quite frankly, I didn't want them to think I was an idiot.

What I failed to realize until that moment was that the successes and failures I've had as an educator and coach have *all* involved my commitment to matters of the heart. Certain relationships with students were easy to fuel and encourage, while others appeared to be running on fumes, without a fill-up station anywhere in sight. At some point, I think we all have been there. But we must intentionally surmount even the difficult moments and invest emotionally, regardless.

Mrs. Brown told me about the culture of my classroom, about how relatable and comfortable I appeared, and about how I was able to form a genuine relationship with her daughter. I had reassured Allie, she said, by being transparent about my own insecurities in math. I made it OK for Allie to feel the stress of her inadequacies and yet continue to press on.

ALL LEARNING IS UNDERSTANDING RELATIONSHIPS

Career educator Rita Pierson has arguably the most moving speech on matters of the heart that I've ever heard. She recalls one educator's response toward empathy: "They don't pay me to like the kids." She replied, "Kids don't learn from people they don't like."

Her TED Talk lasts less than ten minutes. It has over 13 *million* views. Pierson concludes that while poverty, low attendance, and negative peer influences are known accomplices to poor performance, something else is also at work. She spends most of her speech discussing what she calls "the undervalued importance of human connection." She builds on an idea from George Washington Carver that stresses, "All learning is understanding relationships"—a profound statement coming from a scientist.

If I were to challenge you to test this idea of human connection, what would you conclude? What stories would you dredge up as evidence to describe where you are today, for better or worse, and how it directly reflects your past relationships?

The Plutchick Wheel on the next page focuses on emotions, more specifically showing how certain emotions, over time, impact relationships, performance, and behavior.

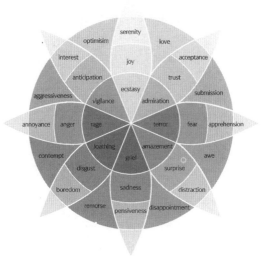

Emotions are complex and move in many directions. When we model emotions and feelings and consider their behavioral implications, we can better prevent emotions from negatively affecting the workplace.[1]

A study, done by Lumen Learning, looks at organizational behavior and aids companies to meet performance goals at the management level by using emotional intelligence as a vehicle to drive home some desired behavior. A key takeaway from this research is simply attitude. A certain attitude toward a person or environment can be determinative. One negative attitude can hurt how a whole group responds to an activity, while one optimistic attitude can inspire wholesale, positive behavioral change—and all on the sole basis of how participants feel toward the individual giving the instruction. The study finds that employees are more likely to remain loyal, remain solutions-driven, and find fulfillment in environments where managers are positive and encouraging.

---

1   https://courses.lumenlearning.com/boundless-management/chapter/drivers-of-behavior/

This revelation is not rocket science. So often, however, we forget that how we feel emotionally, and how our students feel emotionally, plays a vital role in achieving the tasks we have planned. Have we built the type of relationships with our audience required to make our goals both efficient and attainable? It's easier for us to say we have empathy than it is to be intentional about the tools we use to employ empathy. Do we know where to go to emotionally charge ourselves? And can we take our students there?

PROTECT YOUR FIRE

In my early career as an educator, you could usually find me during breaks or at lunch in my classroom being silly with students or on the playgrounds leading some ball game. I rarely visited the staff lounge, for just one reason: subconsciously, I went where I was fed emotionally. The staff lunchroom tended to be a place where educators went to vent.

In some regards, venting isn't a bad thing. Teachers should use each other for support, or when tough lessons or situations occur. Having colleagues willing to hold space for you so that you can vent can feel very encouraging. At the same time, that water-cooler hour can become a whine-fest of negativity.

Teachers don't set out to become the Grinches of education, and yet we can all name "that educational Grinch," the one who finds a complaint in every situation. But even the person you identify as "that guy" or "that woman" did not choose their profession in order to become a Grinch, any more than a student chooses to become a delinquent. Somewhere in the process of using up (or sharing out) gallons of fuel, that coach or teacher has neglected opportunities to refuel so they can get ready for battle again.

We must protect that process. Protect the flame and keep lit your desire to do this work, and as a result, protect your students' desire to show effort and dedication to respond favorably to your benchmark tasks. Like Allie did.

If you desire to protect those flames, you must remain close to your why. Avoid getting drained by people or environments that take you further away from how you are fueled. A book by James Clear titled Atomic Habits suggests that we reflect our environment. Our habits, outlook, performance, and behavior all tend to reflect the environment we inhabit. If we routinely soak in the displeasure of our colleagues' disdain, subconsciously we will bear the same burdens. Fortunately, in my seventeen years of teaching, I have been in many teacher lounges that oozed positive attitudes. We cannot overlook the impact of environment.

As a child living in inner-city Portland, Oregon, I felt attracted to the street life. Had I remained in that environment longer than I did, perhaps it would have pulled me in. In high school, my attraction leaned toward college and sports, more suitable for my new environment in suburbia.

Although my home life didn't push or advocate for higher education, my perspective on success reflected that of my peers and the homes in which they were raised. I learned so many valuable lessons from my friends' parents, although I never received one direct speech. The same was true of some of my teachers. They created environments where academic achievement was just the norm. They routinely reflected possibility and esteem in ways that felt quite foreign to me. Doing well enough academically to play sports in college and earning a degree became an expectation, like breathing, or like the expectation in my home of growing strong spiritually. If any of my peers ventured off this expected path, they would get looked down upon as failures.

My strongest influence was a mentor who routinely spoke words of affirmation. She established such a strong relationship with me that I hung onto her words like we hang on to the last days of summer break. I used her energy and our relationship as fuel to challenge obstacles I routinely faced. In the end, we both found success.

As time went on, I not only thrived as a teacher at Linfield, but I was offered three promotions: Dean of Students, Assistant Principal, and Athletic Director. I took the same insecurities into each role. I can't relate to this dilemma. I'm not qualified to handle this issue. The great truth that I found at Linfield I now bestow upon you:

The greatest tool you can possess in relating to young people is a heart that beats to their ever-changing emotions.

MORE THAN KNOWLEDGE AND CONTENT

If you believe that your mastery of your students' scholastic experience depends solely on your effectiveness at knowledge and content, you will fall short every time. At Linfield Christian School, I did not understand algebra to the degree of confidence I would have liked, but I understood the doubt that rested inside of Allie. I did not understand the economic pressures facing my students, but I understood the emotions of going without. I did not understand what lonely meant through the eyes of a child whose dad worked all the time, but I knew the feelings of deep desolation suffered through loss. I did not know the stress of trying to get into a prestigious college, but I knew the stress associated with school itself. I built relationships from all those perspectives.

I could easily have called this chapter "Emotional Intelligence 2.0," a book co-authored by Travis Bradberry and Jean Greaves. Their book sends readers on an introspective journey that allows them to discover their emotional strengths and weaknesses. Readers obtain vital information that, applied appropriately, allows them to become masters of influence and relationships. In the name of empathy, I believe all educators should spend time looking into this kind of work, because we all fall short at times—not because of a lack of will, but because of a deficiency in skill (see Chapter 5).

KNOW YOUR AUDIENCE

We often praise Hollywood actors and actresses for one skill highlighted in this book. I believe the way an actor connects with a role gives us a model for connecting with our students. Our ability to perform well in the classroom depends on our ability to emotionally connect with our students, even when our journeys contrast.

I remember Will Smith describing his preparation for the role of Muhammad Ali in the movie *Ali*. Will so dedicated himself to his role that he would call Mr. Ali's wife and family just to study behavior, mannerisms, and slang terms. He wanted to learn as much as possible so he could instinctively react and make decisions by understanding the emotions and thought process of Mr. Ali. Will performed masterfully in that role, and I suggest that's not much different from what we would call, in education, a "Master Teacher."

It's our job to know our students so well that we know what stresses them. We anticipate their actions and reactions. We study their character and understand their background. From that place, we understand that while we might not share the same history, we do share the same emotional space. We find commonality and relation there.

That's what it means to be human and to have a heart. It is this truth that allowed me to relate to Linfield students and families, whose physical steps might have seemed very different from mine, but who joined me on the same emotional journey.

REASON FOR CONFIDENCE

I hope that this chapter has reassured you. Perhaps it has given you a sense of confidence to operate relationally in a "foreign" climate. So many educators want to do more, be more, but remain paralyzed by the idea, *I don't have a journey that matches my students' need.*

Although my time at Linfield afforded me little to no opportunities to match steps with my students, it did extend me an opportunity to feel the daily emotions of my students. It also allowed me to find moments in my own journey where I could relate and build authentic relationships with them.

What young people in your life are hoping you would connect with them emotionally and relationally? Do you recognize them? Who are they? Can you name them? They need you to connect your emotions to theirs, not necessarily your experiences or content competence. Mostly, they need your ability to build trust, hope, and possibility, so they can push down whatever hurdles obstruct their journey.

They are silently calling you right now. They need you. Quite frankly, we all do. It's your duty. Will you answer the call?

11

TRUST ACTIVATED THROUGH EMPATHY

I see you, and I see where you can be. Let's go.

BRET UNDERWOOD

What does it look like to activate trust through empathy? When you take a bird's-eye view of the question, or you hear of influencing a child in a positive way, you appreciate the transaction—but can you see the mechanics beneath the operation? Empathetic relationships have intentional action items. Do you know what they are?

By this point in the book, we understand the significant role empathy plays in connecting with our students and having our students connect with us. But using the blanket term "empathy" and describing how it changes student lives can beg the question of how to live it out loud.

Consider the example of coaching, a role most educators can relate to. What elements about that relationship often leave an athlete feeling a deep bond? What part of how you carry yourself as a coach leaves your players inspired to improve as a player and a person? Have you asked them?

I decided to do just that to come up with a definitive answer. I allowed myself to be not merely introspective, but also to search externally for the effective tools of connection. As educators and coaches, we have a sense of when a "normal" relationship transitions to something much deeper, although I am not sure we can pinpoint the exact moment when "it" happens. I imagine that it would prove very puzzling to try to identify when, exactly, your words and actions became a lifeline for your athletes.

I recall a parent telling me, "My son had a tough game. While the team was in the locker room, I knew my son's emotions were going to be really low. I was already preparing the words I could say to lift his spirits. But when he got in the car, he was fine. I asked if he was OK and he said, 'Yes, I called Mr. Broussard in the locker room and he talked to me. I am all good.'"

To a degree, I find that puzzling. What power we have as educators and mentors! Possessing the ability to deflate or inflate the human spirit can be a variable all its own.

I doubt a single response is appropriate for each child. The exact words or action it may take to evoke a certain helpful emotion probably varies—in fact, I know it does, because my success rate at shepherding young minds to excellence comes nowhere close to 100 percent. If the process were easy, would my score go up? Maybe, maybe not. Nevertheless, like many passionate educators, I have had the honor of shepherding my fair share of students, of planting seeds of value and character in their hearts.

To research my own question, I called a few student athletes with whom I've had a special connection. I asked questions that would, I hoped, draw out some secrets to empathy in action. The words and stories I heard humbled me, as I had never before gone looking for the tools I had used to impact young minds. Completing this exercise refreshed me, lifted my spirits, and confirmed my career choice.

If you are a coach or educator, I strongly recommend that you complete a similar exercise. Do so not simply as a cathartic workout, but to affirm your ability to do this work, especially on those down days where you doubt yourself.

My own research found five consistent answers:

Trust activated.

Respect activated.

Consistency activated.

Timeliness activated ("You show up in time of need").

Modeling activated ("You role model your expectations").

THE INTERVIEW PROCESS

I asked each student the same questions, hoping that a conversation would ensue. I wanted to listen to the stories of how and why our interactions morphed from supply and demand into a solid relationship anchored in mentorship and genuine love. You can use the same questions as below, adapt them, or devise new ones, as you explore for yourself what empathy looks like, activated within your own student/teacher relationships.

1. How did it feel when you were inspired?
2. As your coach/mentor, we have endured some trying seasons. What season was the most difficult? Why?
3. Where were you emotionally right before we handled that issue?
4. Why do you think you felt those things?
5. What did I say or do to make you feel hope was still possible?
6. What one statement did I make that you will always remember? Why did that statement have such an effect?
7. What one thing that I've done will you always remember? Why?
8. How did that moment impact the next season of your life?

I'd like you to read the responses I received in the very words used by three student athletes. I hope these responses encourage you to begin or enlarge your own introspective journey and think about your most influential and impactful relationships. How do you think your own students or athletes would answer these questions?

1. **What was our most trying season together?**
    Meghan:
    "Putting the work in and not seeing results. Emotionally, I was frustrated."

    JM:
    "Senior year I had a breakdown because I had a job, basketball, and schoolwork. I just wanted to hustle. I failed to pay attention to the mental health aspects. I wanted to be perfect. I didn't wanna let anyone down. Not my family. I didn't wanna depend on my mom for money. With basketball, I told myself I wanted to play professionally and knew the sacrifice. Academically, I had high standards. They were self-imposed pressures."

    Devin:
    "Right after senior season. I was not getting the looks I wanted."

2. **What did I say or do to make you feel that hope was still possible?**
    Meghan:
    "You were always there. You were very determined. It was the routine. You kept telling me to trust the process; success is found in it. I was embarrassed if I wasn't there because I knew you were. It was inspiring."

Devin:

"You gave me hope. Daily in the gym. Every day in the gym you get 1% better. When we were in the gym you would always tell me, 'you are better than how you are playing.'"

JM:

"You told me you can't let the candle burn at both ends. You were always dedicated and showing up. If you could show up for me, I knew I had to show up for myself. It was a big motivator. Even in college I thought about you often. When things got tough, I knew I couldn't let you down. I remember how you showed up and I was not going to let you down."

3. **How does it feel to be inspired?**

Meghan:

"When my alarm went off at 4:45 a.m., I did not need another alarm. I felt it was my purpose. I was inspired. Before that moment, I knew other people were doing it. I wanted that success."

Devin:

"It feels like there is always someone there for you even when you feel alone. I felt like it was mutual. I did not want to give up because of you."

JM:

"I feel energized to go out and accomplish my goals."

4. What one thing did I say that you will always remember?

Meghan:

"'Suffer the pain of discipline or suffer the pain of regret.' That taught me a lot of self-discipline. It woke me up each day. I would feel bad if I did not get up. You put that type of discipline in me. A student may want to get better, but I think finding the discipline and routine is the gift you gave me."

Devin:

"'It's not easy. If it were easy, everyone would do it.' It stuck with me because it was reality. It was not just basketball. That was life. If I want a good grade or a promotion. If I really want something, it will not be easy, but it is possible. It might be difficult, but it is possible.

"After I had a four- or five-game stretch of bad games, you sent me this text along with a picture of a wolf right before the next game. You sent this over a year ago, when I was in high school, and I still read it before every game even in college. But it is not just sports. It is the mentality for life."

(see next page)

"If I can give u anything it would be this mentality for 32 whole Min. This attitude doesn't dictate a shot attempt every game, a reb every possession. This mindset is simple. Dominate, kill, destroy at every opportunity. There is nothing passive about this mindset. Some have had this mindset and weren't great. But there has never been a great without this mindset. This mindset is bigger than a physical skill. If you prepare your mind, your body will follow. Say a prayer, ask God to give you the gift of a warrior! A fighter, a killer, with the confidence of King David! Don't matter who the Goliath is!!! With a single stone you can slay a giant! Love u and I'm proud of how far you have come. But we are nowhere near your goals! All you have done is prepare..... it's all useless if you don't Kill in battle. Today is battle! Go there mentally. Prepare for battle. And don't confuse that with scoring 40 pts..... simply ATTACK EVERYTHING"

JM:

"'What are you going to put in today? You are not special because you are here. You are special because of what you do when you get here.' That really helped me out mentally, because you knew when I was tired. When I was just going through the motions. So, whenever you said that, it encouraged me to dial back in and give it all I had."

5. What one thing did I do that you will always remember?

Meghan:

"You did the workouts with me. Whatever I did, you did. Your ability to perform the tasks. You were so good and confident with making shot after shot. It made me trust the process.

"You were crazy. You did not drink coffee. I saw how committed you were. You woke up every day. Worked on all these things. And you never stopped."

Devin:

"Your consistent love and support. It wasn't thrown at me or overloaded. It was just consistent.

"You drove me to Vanguard University for my college tryout. It had a great impact. It told me you really cared. When my mom and dad were going through a divorce, you told me that you would always be around. It made me feel like I will always have a family. I can always come to you.

"Visualizing exercise. Before one session, you had me lie on the ground and close my eyes. You had me visualize my training and the game at the same time. You had me go through the steps of the game in my mind as you walked around me reminding me what I have put in. What the game really is. When you were speaking, those images popped up in my head. That really helped.

"It was just something different. I never experienced anything like that. It helped me get my mind right. Regardless of the environment around you, you have to stick to your roots. What I work on is what I work on. Nothing changes. The only thing different is the environment."

JM:

"My senior year I transferred back into school with no real contacts for college ball. When I said I wanted to play for UC Santa Cruz, you called the coach. Got me a tryout. When I said I did not have money to go, you helped fund-raise for me. You helped me physically prepare. Mentally prepare. You went with me, which was a big help. That whole experience was just the biggest thing anyone has ever done for me.

"From the outside looking in, I noticed how many good relationships you had with other classmates. That meant a lot to me. I knew that was rare. It was not just me that you had a relationship with. It told me that you were genuine in making a change and affecting people. Your influence has a wide range. It is not just for a few people. It is inspiring. Seeing you do what you do made me want to use my abilities to influence and inspire as well."

6. **How did the season we shared impact you in your next season of life?**

Meghan:

"Something you have impacted me on now is purpose. Thirsty for more. I want to be inspired. I am looking for that. When I was with you, I was so fulfilled. I knew my purpose. I was excited about the work. Without that purpose, you feel empty and going in circles.

"You never asked me for anything. All the training. All the time we shared, five-plus days a week, you never asked me for anything. You were not training me for money; I was simply a kid who needed guidance, and you were there. That really stood out and inspired me to give back to the next generation."

Devin:

"My confidence. Because of my work ethic and training and how we prepared, I felt like I had an advantage on everybody. When college first started, I was busy and my schedule was challenging. But after a few weeks, I knew I needed the work and it was easy for me to dial back into all the dedication and training we did."

JM:

"It gave me an understanding of how much work is needed. It gave me an understanding of what type of environment I need to be in. Before I met you, I would say I wanted to be a professional player and play in college. Then when I was exposed to the exact things to do, I was not even close to working hard enough to accomplish my goals before meeting you. Now I know the work ethic needed to achieve my other goals. I can take the lessons from basketball and transfer that process to film."

7. **What's the most vital thing you would tell a child influencer about mentorship?**

Meghan:

"Don't be discouraged by kids' reactions to you. Teachers can get discouraged about how teenagers respond. Young. Immature. Rude. Do not react. Stay consistent."

Devin:

"Always be there. Does not matter what situation."

JM:

"The relationship must be rooted in mutual respect. Every great relationship I have had with a teacher or coach started with them respecting me enough to listen to me and valuing my opinion, and me doing the same for them."

MENTORING FUTURE MENTORS

Do you know the irony of all of this? When I was the age of these students, I found myself in the throes of my own journey. I felt very insecure about my prospects as a fourteen-year-old. I remember not necessarily doubting my ability to succeed, but rather doubting the resources I had to achieve success.

In some ways, I felt like I was going it all alone. I wanted to live in a house, I wanted a family structure that looked like that of my friends. I wanted financial stability something close to that of my classmates. Lacking those realities, I was fortunate enough to have a mentor of my own. Her name was Michele Silvestri.

I thought of Michele as I read the responses of my students. What was it about her that allowed me to have wings? What energy did she provide that allowed me to activate greatness at levels I didn't see in me or around me? Our worlds contrasted as much as did our nationalities. I was an inner-city kid adrift in suburbia, floating like a misplaced branch in a big pond. She was an Italian American who, if it weren't for her name and occasional accent, would pass as your typical white educator from upstate New York. She preferred hikes and nature. I preferred basketball and Naughty by Nature. She was books and Saturday markets; I was magazines and the fashion market. She routinely leaned into me, as I routinely found her world annoying.

Admittedly, it was a humorous annoyance. We shared a deep bond with one another, much like what I have with my students. She would laugh about forcing me to do things outside my comfort zone. Behind my complaints, I would secretly relish the opportunity to learn a whole new world.

In typical Michele fashion, for one of my birthdays she gifted me a picture in a frame that I keep in my office to this day. It wasn't a picture of Magic Johnson or Kobe Bryant or anything I would have picked for myself. Nope, it was a picture of the Grand Canyon. Greater than the picture, though, was the note she wrote on its back. She told me how big the world was, if only my vision would extend further than my eyesight. She told me she believed in me and how confident she was that I was going to make it, whatever "it" was. She was to me what I was to Meghan, Devin, JM, and multiple students over my seventeen-year career.

I'm still not sure what Michele saw in me to make her keep showing up as she did, but I am glad she did. Even if she did not know the exact words to say, her words always proved she cared. Even if she did not understand exactly my world, she was always willing to show me hers, and by doing so it opened my eyes to more diverse opportunities than the ones available to me in my own neighborhood. She helped save me, and the work I do daily reflects her spirit and her ability to help others identify and activate their own work.

Michele was that one caring adult who helped create success in me and through me. She consistently and always poured life into me. She poured hope inside a hopeless container, reconfiguring possibility inside my impossible world.

LESSONS THROUGH LOSSES

I hope that reading these stories has brought you some epiphany, some aha moments, or perhaps your inner light bulb found its "on" switch. The perspectives of my students lack exact coordinates as much as they highlight emotional connection.

I chose diverse experiences and stories because empathy doesn't work well if we mentor from an automated space. We must resist the temptation to follow a world that insists, "if Johnny gets two orange slices, then Sally also must get two orange slices." That is not empathy activated. Empathy requires addressing the individual, not necessarily measuring out a single, "equal" solution.

I have failed miserably at times because I automated my empathy response. As a result, the influence and the connection I wanted simply didn't happen. I used the same measures of success, imagining that it would bring me the same result. It brought the opposite.

My failed attempts taught me the same lesson that coaches learn every year all across our country: *every opponent is different.* As a basketball coach, I found success playing full-court defense when we faced a bigger and slower opponent. I would be foolish to think the same tactic would work against a smaller and quicker opponent. My game plan had to morph, to focus on half-court defense to counter their speed, making it less likely we would give up easy layups.

As a young coach I failed often whenever I took the same mental approach toward every situation. I wanted to get my students so fired up and inspired that they would run through walls. When I coached in Alaska, I had a player—our best player—quit right in the middle of a playoff game. We were the number-one seed, in a tight battle late in the game. During a timeout, I gave a classic rah-rah speech about how big the moment was, about how we trained so hard, about how everything was on us to deliver. It was something to behold. Surely, every yelling coach in America would have been proud.

But when we broke our huddle, our best player never got off the bench. This confused our players. The other team also looked puzzled, but delighted. I tried to tell my player to get in the game; he didn't even look up at me. He just shook his head, slumped in fright, staring at a puddle of sweat. I knew what had happened because it had happened before. The pressure got to him. I got to him. I made the moment bigger than it really was, even though I knew his past and his triggers. And he froze. Some might call it performance anxiety. I call it putting him in a position that brought out flashbacks of failures and the feared repercussions of not being great.

We lost the game. But far more importantly, I lost my player. The season ended, and in some ways, so did my relationship with my player. Things never seemed to fall back in place following that night.

Automated responses to empathy simply don't work, at least not in the way we want them to. In this case, my automated approach to emotionally connect with a kid "worked," but in the wrong way. I had hoped to use emotion to bring out the best in my player; instead, I drove him toward an emotional meltdown.

We can all recall similar stories where we just miss it. I can count plenty of times in the classroom, on the court, or in the office where I had hoped to enlighten a young person and make an empathic connection, but instead found rejection. I understand that sometimes we just don't connect with a student. Our words don't connect, our actions seem forced. It happens, like in baseball. We swing, we miss. We swing, we hit. That's the game. As batters, though, we learn. We grow as we realize that each pitcher and each pitch is different. Timing, aggression, and swings must change with every new pitch. Do you know when I really fail? I fail most often when my "swing" with a student is automated, predetermined, taken without consciously studying whatever is coming my way.

Taking action that prompts self-growth in young people should force educators to look at each child's problems as a new pitch, a new opponent. The constant is us wanting to be of service to these children during their time of need. That's *always* the same. It's why we compete in and choose to fight within this profession. If we decide on our game plan after we truly study our opponent—if we observe and analyze the challenge facing our students, along with who they are as individuals—we might realize that although Johnny received two orange slices, Sally might require something different. Maybe she needs a banana, because oranges might trigger something in her, causing her to react in an adverse way. But the only way to know *that* is to get to know Sally.

KEYS TO SUCCESS

Even though the right solutions may vary for each child, the following attitudes must infuse every action item if we are to encourage every relationship toward its optimal state. Regardless of the relationship—educator, coach, administrator, mentor—the following elements all must be present if we are to press forward.

Respect

For a child to become willing to respond, we must offer respect, including both our verbal and nonverbal communication. In the short term, a child may play along if the desired goal seems within reach; but long-term relationship effectiveness requires respect to be given and received.

Consistency

Inspiration lasts only so long. When the emotion fades, our promises must remain. Inky Johnson, a motivational speaker and influencer, says, "Commitment is staying true to what you said you would do long after the mood that you said it in has left." Having the discipline to keep showing up every day is the lifeline of life change. Without consistency, we eventually lose every relationship we hold dear.

Timeliness

Storms happen. They come at unpredictable times. No one can ever schedule or postpone a storm . . . just like mentorship. Urgencies may at times keep us from getting to the storms our young people face, but from the macro level, we must remain prepared and willing to respond whenever our young people send us an SOS. We must show up when it matters most.

Role modeling

A pastor once said the greatest sermon we will ever give is the one we preach without using our lips. To change our audience's perspective from wonder to possibility, we must show them the way. Show them we are, have been, and will walk them through whatever transformation they need. Our words remain empty unless we *go there* with them. We must be what we preach.

Trust

Trust comes in levels, and it takes time to reach the level of trust needed to get big results. Start small and be consistent. Your greatest value will always be your dependability during unstable seasons. Don't undo with one word or action what it took months and years to build. Young people hang onto your words, until continued broken promises render them useless. If they can't trust who *you* are, they won't hear who you say *they* are. A lack of trust creates doubt about the wings you say they have; and even if they believe they have those wings, they will doubt their wings are meant for flying. Do all that you can to get your students in the air and keep them there.

ONE CARING ADULT

Josh Shipp is an award-winning speaker and author. His work highlights his time as an at-risk youth in foster care and how he has turned his life's mission into helping families, schools, and youth agencies navigate the complexities of overcoming childhood adversities. His books target adults and adolescents while breaking down the formula of influence. Although I highly recommend you look into his body of work, I want to save you hours of reading by spotlighting his most pertinent phrase:

"Every kid is one caring adult away from being a success story."

I couldn't help but think about Shipp's famous line and knowing, without a doubt, that JM, Meghan, and Devin are success stories because, in their cases, I was that one caring adult. Did they have other caring adults in their lives who helped shape them? Absolutely. But I am the only adult over whom I have control.

Just as you are the only adult over whom you have control.

The students highlighted in this chapter are fortunate enough to have been "raised by a village." Moms, dads, coaches, primary- and secondary-level teachers, all play a hand in this process. We are the village, we are the team, and at some point, the ball is in each of our hands. It's our job to send it down the right path so that each child can find their real win. In every village, each adult must take turns lending what they do best in hopes that they help young people identify what *they* do best and pursue that best version of themselves each day.

Our students, their interests, and their storms vary—unique as every human fingerprint. The journey of each child will be a beautiful star, a single snowflake, or a solitary wave that comes to your shore at its own speed, in its own shape, and demanding its own appreciation. If we compare one star's brilliance to any other star in the sky, its radiance may dim into darkness, forever. So, let's study each star. Let's fuel each one with whatever it needs to shine. And then, let's watch as it blazes a brilliant trail across the sky, finding its own glorious destiny.

12

JUST A PARTY

*Be bold enough to use your voice, brave enough to listen to your heart,
and strong enough to live the life you have always imagined.*

ANONYMOUS

I sat atop a utility road above the Murrieta Mesa High School stadium football field, looking up at the crescendo of fireworks exploding over my head. The culmination of the school's ten-year anniversary, the football game, our ascension to relevance, how we have found our identity, how far we've come—all found their climax at that moment. Each explosion of color served as a flashbang of the memories and hurdles it took to arrive. You might think of it as an aesthetic functioning as physical nostalgia, if that's a thing.

Filling the stands below, thousands of stories stood tall. They all gazed at the sparkle in the sky and at the wonder within. Lining the track were past alumni and former difference-makers uniting as a single idea, possibility, and promise fulfilled. They were the ones who built the walls, opened the first books, and held the first letterman jackets emblazoned with school identity markers. They stood in the same end zone as brothers, teammates, and opponents, inhaling deep breaths of finality and competition.

As with any athlete, then began the mental assessment of opportunities missed and moments captured. Critiquing the arrival of the moment and finding pride dressed in the effort collectively harnessed by both teams, I can confidently say that peace radiated within the huddle. I will never forget it. In fact, it served as a closing chapter for anyone there that night who sacrificed something in hopes of creating an amazing school and community. The whole day was a celebration, a party, intentionally orchestrated in hopes that it would both honor the tradition as it stands now and cast new dreams for future Rams.

Months later, as I continued to revel in the significance of the moment, both for me personally and for the school collectively, someone in my inner circle who should have been aware made a comment that I will never forget.

"It was just a party!" he said.

For a moment, re-read the paragraphs above and notice how the scene described was anything but "just a party." *What would cause a person to say that,* I wondered. That moment was anything but "just a party" for the thousands who gathered that day. The statement completely jarred me. *The audacity,* I thought. *And the gall, especially considering who said it!*

I realized, eventually, that the truly inept and emotionally fragile one was *me.*

At the end of the day, we alone truly understand the vital moments in our lives and their significance. Such confirming, transformative moments can be drawn only from within. *Never* let the opinions of others form your beliefs about what you overcame, about your dreams, or about your calling.

If the journey of life is about the moments in between the mile markers, and not the finality of the ride, then it would be perfectly acceptable for someone to have a different view than you do. When their only experience of your journey was your ending point, or they had experienced only one of the many mileposts of your perilous trek, how could they *not* have a differing view?

Unfortunately, such a perspective can feel extremely dangerous and puzzling, often frightening us and sometimes paralyzing our convictions. We tend to sell short the lessons learned and convictions felt as mile markers pile up, for fear that we might be *seen*, truly seen. As pedestrians inevitably line the roads of our lives, like observers witnessing a marathon, it's paramount to remember that they pitch their tent in a different place than our own. It sits in only one moment in time. For spectators standing near the finish line, your exuberance and over-the-top celebration and joy may be seen as "weird," "overblown," or perhaps, "just a party." They cannot know that you began your race in difficulty, defeat, and desperation.

Your plight has produced an emotional callus that often gets covered up (but it remains). Thus is born the challenge and the commission. As an igniter of young minds, the tools and places you must go, while remaining emotionally transparent, must often be used during times suffocated by the fear of false perceptions and a lack of understanding on the part of the world around you. I plead with you now, for the sake of brighter minds and the advancement of our communities, fear no one who judges you for being uniquely you. Only then can the ones you serve find a space that is uniquely theirs.

I'm completely aware that someone who failed to go through the emotional trauma I suffered as a child may view my compassion for young people as "different" or "extra." So, in order to stay on mission, I decided long ago that I must accept that not everyone will understand my purpose. That's true for you, too. Only you define your journey and what it means.

As an example, I think of my brother, who I spoke about in Chapters 7 and 9. I described his life as a reckless teenager and how each step forward provided evidence that his life had no ultimate meaning or purpose. What I didn't say is how he allowed others to define his circumstances for him. When we allow others to define us by our circumstances, we subconsciously allow them to influence us, shaping how we respond to our current situation.

At some point, or shall I say, as he neared some significant mileposts along his journey, my brother realized that the life he was living wasn't authentically his. His reckless behavior and drive for destruction grew out of a license given to him by influencers, who made it OK for him to view his adversity as unfair. They saw his sad plight and encouraged him to adopt a victim mentality—and all of his decisions flowed out of this flawed perspective. They made it OK for him to think that his poor decisions were merely acceptable responses to his difficult circumstances, even though his path led to personal destruction.

Divinity saw to it, however, that my brother began to find reasons to stop imploding and instead start changing, igniting. He thought he had a good reason for raging as he did, until one day he understood that the emotional license people had handed him was not in his best interest. He boldly started to repurpose all the emotions and experiences he faced. He changed his perspective, and when he did, his purpose changed along with it.

He had to understand that he was much more than a victim, the same way I understood Mesa's Legacy Bowl was much more than "just a party." He stopped allowing others to define his journey and instead started to define it for himself. At that moment, he allowed himself to own his story and respond to the world from a victor's mindset.

Today, he serves not only as a mentor and success coach for me, but also does the same thing for several companies and top-level executives around the country. By choosing to break the bondage that others had influenced him to take on, he began to discover how he authentically felt about the obstacles he faced and what they meant for him. That journey of self-discovery led him to start his "Life Repurposed" company and lifestyle brand. The moment he decided to define for himself the meaning and purpose for each milepost of his life, he started to change lives around him for the better.

This is an Open letter to my big bro
I am who I am
Cause you showed me where to go

You owned yo mistakes
You a changed man
Now you do whatever it takes
To change men

Yep I'm noticing
Taking mental notes and blueprints
...You my foreman
I watch as close now, as I did before man
Insert from *Diary of a Poet,* "Open letter to my big bro"

IT'S YOUR JOURNEY, NO ONE ELSE'S

If you want to be truly authentic, if you desire to have genuine influence, you cannot filter your perspective through someone else's narrative. Their journey is not yours. Their gifting is not yours. Their calling and purpose are not yours. All of us have tints and hues and colors unique to us alone. It's your responsibility to talk about *your* perspective.

Don't lose sight of your purpose. Don't make small and toss to the wayside experiences intended as foundations of hope with the power to encourage others to hang on just a little longer. Be brave enough to refuse to allow individuals who you were not meant to influence, overshadow those who cling to your perspective like a lifeline. We must have strength enough to ignore the white noise and focus on the quiet whisper inside our hearts, begging us to heal and help make whole the communities we serve.

Just know that the greater your convictions, the louder the background racket grows. Regardless of where that white noise comes from—whether from colleagues, students, friends, peers, or family—we must withstand the onslaught of insecurity, doubt, and negativity. It's all a part of the ride.

For me, I had to focus on where Mesa started and where it had been. After the words "it was just a party" caused me emotional distress, I had to recalibrate my energy and focus on what really mattered. I had to focus on this defining moment as a result of the school's amazing journey.

A commonly-used idiom goes, "We lost our way." The phrase defines a particular part of a journey or season. To a degree, "our way" at Mesa, both collectively and as a community, was never truly established, recognized, or appreciated, largely as a result of being the newest educational institution in the area. Our community is extremely competitive in athletics. As one rival athletic director exclaimed, "Athletics will always be the front porch to any school, because it's the most visible."

With that understanding, it's not hard to see how the community perceived the new Mesa brand. We didn't have a lot of early success. In fact, a large contingency of coaches and staff tried hard to re-assign Mesa athletics to a less-competitive league, in hopes that we could "be more successful."

Fast forward four years to this moment, to the fireworks

exploding over our stadium. We had completely shifted the relevancy landscape in our area. Mesa athletes were performing at an all-time high, including winning state championships in various sports. Our student section was recognized as the most spirited in all of southern California. Our campus was adorned with shiny aesthetics celebrating our athletic excellence. The school's enrollment numbers had reached historic marks, with a waiting list to get in.

We had arrived . . . or at the very least, we grew. And the entire community had taken notice.

Thus, our Legacy Bowl was very timely. The stars aligned for us to celebrate our "arrival" and our ten-year anniversary at the same time. Yes, it was much *more* than a party!

I thought about all the faculty, students, and families who had sacrificed and helped build such an amazing school. This was their moment to reflect on and appreciate their accomplishment. Personal journeys, along with a community of pride, radiated throughout Ram stadium that night.

And so, I sat atop the stadium and tailored this moment for myself. I understood all too well its improbability. Fewer than twenty percent of students performing below grade level in elementary school ever graduate college. Only twelve percent of teens between the ages of fourteen and sixteen living in a single-parent home go on to earn a degree, compared to thirty-eight percent of two-parent homes. Only fifty-eight percent of students who spend one to three years in foster care ever graduate from high school, and half of those students end up homeless or in jail after they graduate.

I can rattle off statistic after statistic, highlighting why my checkered past should have prevented me from waving a checkered flag signaling my victory lap. Those thoughts swept into my mind all at once, like an avalanche. I went from being a low-performing student to an overachieving professional with two master's degrees. I accepted a position as an assistant principal by the age of thirty, knowing full well the average age of a school administrator was forty-five. I went from public embarrassment and scrutiny to public praise and pride when I was selected as a top-10 Athletic Director in the country in back-to-back years (2017-18 and 2018-19). I spent a lifetime camouflaging the fragility of my emotional health, hoping to be an unseen speck amongst thousands.

Now, I sat atop my perch, having helped to give a transfusion of heart to an array of wandering spirits, joyously radiating around the stadium below. I went from an insecure, mute voice to a trumpet of confidence. The strength of my spirit has served as a billboard of possibility for young journeymen moving onward from milepost to milepost. I have an improbable life. I don't feel deserving of the blessings and favor connected to it.

As the fireworks continued to explode above my head, I observed each sparkle and flash in the evening sky. Each of them made me feel incredibly humbled. I know for sure this was not all my doing, and I will honor the favor bestowed upon me by making sure I continue to pay it forward, one person at a time.

THE PARTY OF A LIFETIME

If this "Legacy Bowl" were really just a party, then for me it was the party of a lifetime. What I refused to do then is what I encourage you to do now. I didn't allow the perception of one person to stagger my belief in my purpose, and I urge you to remain strong in your commitment to your own mission.

Because you chose a vocation of service, deep inside you lives the drive to nurture those around you. This energy births ideas for

178

real impact. The only way to maximize your influence, however, is to understand the origins of your calling.

First, where does your conviction come from? Do you know? Second, what experiences have you faced that have shaped your perspective and aim? Arming yourself with this knowledge allows you to intentionally get to work. More importantly, it helps protect the "party poopers" from taking hold of your principles and spoiling them.

As an educator, you have deep convictions about reaching out to students, starting a project, or speaking out against educational inequalities. As a coach, you have clarity over the performance or achievement of a player or team. You know what personal success looks like, regardless of what the score reads. You have an internal barometer on progress that spectators often fail to appreciate. Understanding the growth and arrival of these moments elevates our satisfaction and appreciation for our students and our service to them.

By all means necessary, protect your vocational fulfillment. Yes, it's a battle! Too often, gifted educators and coaches fall short of pursuing their true convictions, either because of someone else's false sense of success, or by allowing themselves to judge success or purpose by some external definition. Such a mindset routinely stunts our ability to move fluidly within our purpose, with both determination and desire. It thwarts us from making any attempt to resurrect, rescue, and restore the young souls we desire to see set free and blazing brightly.

Remember, it's your party. Only you can truly decide the theme. Now, party on!

YOU MUST GO BACK TO TAKE THEM FORWARD

People don't burn out because of what they do.
People burn out because life makes them forget why they do it.

INKY JOHNSON

While our journeys differ, our hearts beat the same. You must look inside yourself, reflect on the pain, the comfort, the isolation and inclusion, and retrace ways in which feelings of peace replaced worry. I hope you stay in that space and never retreat or retire from it.

The idea of dwelling in a constant state of agony or despair, rather than simply remaining sensitive to all the things you have felt and why, can never heal others. You must resurrect your own emotions if you are to take your students where they need to go. You must go back to take them forward. The idea here is not to forget the pain behind our experiences, it is to make peace with it. Wholeness is not cutting off parts of who we are, it is the opposite. It is embracing all of who we are and using emotional cues to make healthy decisions.

Unfortunately, our society does not teach this truth. Instead, it urges us to forget, move on, ignore. By packing away certain emotions, however (usually the "negative" ones), we also pack away the empathy we need to give light to the very thing we're here to serve.

I assure you, your service is greatly needed! Will you answer the call?

You have young people in your path who cry out to you in silence, hoping to be seen, rescued, and shown a new and positive path. Will you have eyes to see and ears to hear? Will you have a heart to respond, or will apathy overtake the place where empathy used to reside? Life will provide more than enough deterrents to desensitize the places in your soul where compassion once reigned.

Be resilient for the sake of the Sarahs, Devins, and Dylans in your own world. As an educator, you write your own story every day. Encounter by encounter, pages are being filled by the way you choose to respond to each plea of each precious student.

May your story be grand!

The monotony of our job requirements and the politics of "meeting standards" often rob us of our zest. They blind us from the call we answered. They can bring bondage and steal the passion we once pledged to give to young people. We thus rob the hearts of the young, leaving them void of possibility and hope during their trials. How much better to help turn their trials into triumphs!

A healthy emotional ecosystem enables a young person to become victorious, and this ecosystem's most vital conduit is you. The vitality of their lives depends on the vitality of your perspective. And so, I urge you to stay securely fastened in the original spark that lit the flame, the spark that powered your dreams to do this work in the first place. To lose that perspective is to lose your purpose, and ultimately to lose your soul.

We hear many stories about professional athletes. On the outside, we fantasize about the glamor of such a lifestyle. To perform in front of millions each year? To travel on private jets, sleep in hotels befitting royalty, be treated like kings and queens?

How marvelous! The reality is, however, that athletes also struggle. The longer the career, the easier it is to lose passion. Travel becomes a burden, constant media attention becomes intrusive, maintaining a polished image becomes suffocating, and fighting for the next contract becomes stressful. The politics of professional athletics often turns into an engine driving a vehicle in which the athlete no longer wishes to ride. At this T in the road, most athletes must decide: retire or rediscover?

Before the public evaluation of their athletic abilities, before the constant media attention, before the drowning political implications of such a lifestyle, there was simply . . . joy. The bounce, the catch, the kick—each sport is unique, but the common emotion where it started for all athletes is the same: passion. Who can describe the rush of energy created in the moment of competition and adrenaline? Nothing else matters. A loss, a win, a good performance, a bad performance, it all triggers a singular response: "rest up, and do it again tomorrow." Their heart beats for a single purpose, and their only wish is to stay in that competitive euphoria for as long as possible. The rebirth of that spirit allows for direction and provides an anchor, a loud retort against the politics that too often foil the beauty of their passion for the sport.

Desensitization impacts how all dedicated professionals— whether cops, doctors, lawyers, firefighters, athletes, or others—feel about the experiences they have and the situations into which they get placed. According to Bruce Perry and Maia Szalavitz, authors of *Born for Love,* repeated exposure to some situation decreases our sensitivity to that experience. Their book outlines a medical study focused on pre-med students that found a significant decrease in empathy in doctors after year three. Deliberate work must be done, they say, for doctors to remain emotionally responsive, for them to protect the idea that the *people* they care for require as much attention as the *aid* these doctors give.

The world of education is no different. Serving young people is no different than serving patients. Therefore, wherever you are in your career, I challenge you to find that center. Find that correlation. You have a duty to whatever platform you chose. Your why is the spirit in which you perform the service, not the service itself. If you cannot identify your why, then you are not truly alive in what you are doing. You may be breathing, but I assure you, you are not alive. And if you are not alive, then you cannot give life to others. It's impossible.

As Dr. Martin Luther King famously penned, "darkness cannot drive out darkness; only light can do that. Hate cannot drive out hate; only love can do that." I, too, have a few proverbs that I'd like to use to charge you now:

> Apathy cannot not drive out apathy; only empathy can do that.
> Hopelessness cannot drive out hopelessness; only hope can do that.
> A lost child cannot spark a lost child to greatness; only you can do that.
> So be bold. Be loud. Be seen. I realize I can't save any lives unless I expose my soul.

Suppose that one day you feel some trepidation about your involvement in civil rights advocacy. If you speak out against injustice, the possibility of trouble coming your way becomes a certainty. A stranger sitting beside you, however, tells you that your greatest bondage is the fear inside you, and that true freedom rests in your unwavering spirit. He says the pain of a confined spirit will far supersede that of your body in chains.

Still, you have little faith, and so you cast doubt on the wisdom you just heard. What happens? Your quandary remains. *What does this man know, anyway*, you think. Before moving on with your day, you thank him and ask for his name, just to be courteous.

"Nelson Mandela," he says.

Your eyes pop. You feel overcome with embarrassment as you realize he's not only been where you have been, but he made it out, to the very top. And in no time at all, wonder replaces embarrassment.

That is the spirit that I hope underlies the writing of this book. That also is the spirit in which I encourage you to write yours. We cross paths daily with young people who hear our words but who will remain forever unmoved until they know our story. I doubt that any of us walk around, looking for opportunities to show vulnerability. It's not human nature to do so. But it is necessary if young people are to thrive; and the more you do it, the more comfortable you become in that space. Understanding the critical nature of it all, I choose to march on, by any means necessary.

Will you march on with me?

I cannot bear to think of finding a young person trapped in the middle of life's battles, and yet leaving them struggling there, potentially forever, while I have the tools to offer aid. When I look at our youth, I want to remember what it feels like to be them, the same way as those who came before me remember what it felt like to be me. I encourage you to do the same thing.

Marshal your pain, your dark days and nights, whatever was taken or lost, and use those things to force your heart to beat in a new way. Embrace this process. Allow it to birth in you new direction and fresh passion for empathy, and then allow that empathy to heal the world around you. As you find others to heal, you also will find a new you—renewed, confident, and courageous.

Ultimately, that is the most qualified display of empathy: to understand someone's else's path by simply and truly embracing your own.